MARDI GRAS TREASURES

FLOAT DESIGNS OF THE GOLDEN AGE

MARDI GRAS TREASURES

FLOAT DESIGNS OF THE GOLDEN AGE

Henri Schindler

PELICAN PUBLISHING COMPANY
Gretna 2001

This book is dedicated to the memory of Louis Andrews Fischer (1901-1974).

*The word "Pelican" and the depiction of a pelican are trademarks
of Pelican Publishing Company, Inc., and are registered
in the U.S. Patent and Trademark Office.*

Library of Congress Cataloging-in-Publication Data

Schindler, Henri.
    Mardi Gras treasures : float designs of the Golden Age / Henri Schindler.
       p. cm.
    Includes index.
    ISBN 1-56554-723-3 (hc : alk. paper)
    1. Carnival floats—Louisiana—New Orleans—History. 2. Carnival floats—Louisiana—New
Orleans—Design and construction. 3. Parade float designers—Louisiana—New Orleans. 4.
Carnival—Louisiana—New Orleans—History. I. Title.

GT4211.N4 S37 2001
791.6—dc21

2001021543

Page 1: *Seigneurjan and Giroux, "Le Carnaval et March Burlesque du Boeuf Gras," procession of the Boeuf Gras, Paris, circa 1830. Engraving by Porret.*
Page 2: *Bror Anders Wikstrom, "Comus, No. 1 Car," watercolor float design for Comus pageant, 1890: "The Palingenesis of the Mistick Krewe."*
Page 3: *Jennie Wilde, "The River of Night," tracing of watercolor float design for Comus pageant, 1904: "Izdubar."*
Page 5: *Charles Briton, "Indian Elephant," watercolor design for papier-mâché walking figure in Comus pageant, 1873: "The Missing Links to Darwin's Origin of Species."*
Page 6: *Seigneurjan and Giroux, "Le Carnaval et March Burlesque du Boeuf Gras," procession of the Boeuf Gras, Paris, circa 1830. Engraving by Porret.*

Printed in Korea
Published by Pelican Publishing Company, Inc.
1000 Burmaster Street, Gretna, Louisiana 70053

CONTENTS

INTRODUCTION

Among the numerous felicities that have made New Orleans the least American of American cities, none surpass, in age or affection, the joys of Carnival. The glimmering processions of the masked gods and bearded kings of the New Orleans Carnival occupy a central position among the rites and glories of the great festival. And more: nothing better illustrates the worldly old city's fabled decadence or extravagant sensibility. The long succession of these glowing, torch-lit pageants—with their towering monsters and fantastic décors, their papier-mâché kingdoms and diamond-dust thrones—became the greatest and most beloved of New Orleans communal rituals.

Following the Louisiana Purchase in 1803, the governing of Creole Louisiana became young America's first experience in governing a foreign country. Masquerade balls and Mardi Gras masking, established customs in New Orleans, were viewed with disdain and worry by the American powers; the *Gazette* became the city's first English-language newspaper in 1823 and editorialized the following year: "As New Orleans has been famous for keeping out enemies of our republic, we cannot conceive why it should permit a gate for the introduction of this rotten relic of European degeneracy." Protestant Anglo-America, having won a great battle against the British a mere decade earlier in New Orleans, solemnly went about the business of securing its Manifest Destiny. However, the Creoles of Louisiana possessed none of the American passions for revolution, democracy, or progress; their colonial status may have ended with the Purchase, but Creole cultural allegiances remained unabashedly French and Catholic, and the relics of Europe were held dear.

An insatiable appetite for music and parades permeated nineteenth-century New Orleans. Parades with marching bands were frequently staged by the city's numerous benevolent societies, fire companies, and military organizations; funeral processions were already an established custom when Benjamin Latrobe, writing in *Appearance of New Orleans in 1819*, called them "peculiar alone to New Orleans among American cities." Latrobe also noted, "As it is now the Carnival, every evening is closed with a ball, a play, or a concert."

The early Creole Carnival was a season of festivities and masquerades that began every year on Twelfth Night, the Feast of Epiphany, and culminated with numerous masked balls, public and private, on Mardi Gras night. There was little gaiety and no Mardi Gras in the uptown American sector, but on Mardi Gras the streets of the old Creole city were transformed into a magical, carefree, open-air theater and parade ground. On this final day of Carnival, maskers from every walk of life cavorted with joyous abandon, for the following day was always Ash Wednesday, the beginning of the Lenten season of penance and fasting.

Maj. James R. Creecy, writing years later in *Scenes in the South, and Other Miscellaneous Pieces,* recalled the Mardi Gras of 1835: "Men and boys, women and girls, bond and free, white and black, yellow and brown, exert themselves to invent and appear in grotesque, quizzical, diabolical, horrible, strange masks and disguises. Human bodies are seen with heads of beasts and birds, beasts and birds with human heads; demi-beasts, demi-fishes, snakes heads and bodies with arms of apes; man-bats from the moon; mermaids; satyrs, beggars, monks, and robbers parade and march on foot, on horseback, in wagons, carts, coaches . . . in rich profusion up and down the streets, wildly shouting, singing, laughing, drumming, fiddling, fifeing, and all throwing flour broascast as they wend their reckless way."

The year 1837 brought the first mention of a Mardi Gras parade by the press, in the new American paper, the *Picayune*. The larger display of the following year was applauded by Creole and American papers. *La Créole* announced, "The whole town doubled up with laughter . . . the beautiful and joyous cavalcade wound its way at full speed. . . . What noise! What hubbub! And what fun." The *Picayune* declared:

> The grand cavalcade which passed through the principal streets was an entertaining sight—being remarkable for numbers, for the splendor of their equipage, and the ludicrous effect which they produced . . . great pains were taken to get up the

affair in proper style. A large number of young gentlemen, principally Creoles of the first respectability, went to no little expense with their preparations. In the procession were several carriages superbly ornamented—personations of knights, cavaliers, heros, demigods, chanticleers, and punchinellos, all mounted. Many of them were dressed in female attire, and acted the lady with no small degree of grace.

The young Creoles who organized these early marches modeled their efforts on the Mardi Gras they had enjoyed as students in Paris, and like the raucous procession of Parisian maskers, the New Orleans parades were noted more for their joie-de-vivre than for organization or artistry. The cavalcade of 1841 was preceded by announcements in the press, and thousands of maskers and spectators lined the streets and crowded the cast-iron balconies to view the "Bedouins." Louis Fitzgerald Tasistro, an Irish actor and writer, was in the city for Mardi Gras:

> There was one remarkable feature connected with the celebration which is strongly characteristic of that love for the embellishments and elegances of life which prevades all the better class of Creoles. This was a procession, composed of between two and three hundred of the first gentlemen of the city, all dressed as Bedouin Arabs, and forming altogether one of the most imposing sights I ever beheld. . . . When Carnival frolics are made subservient to the display of so much taste as was evinced on this occasion, folly is indeed wisdom.

New Orleans was becoming a great seaport and her population had grown from 8,000 at the time of the Louisiana Purchase in 1803 to 145,000 by the mid-1840s. The old Creole sector enjoyed this prosperity, which saw the construction of grand residences, shops, and the stately St. Louis Hotel. But American entrepreneurs controlled most of the city's commerce, and as their numbers and their fortunes increased, they moved farther uptown, to what became called the Garden District. Unlike the Creole houses, which opened onto the sidewalks, and whose gardens were enclosed in courtyards, the

Garden District mansions were in the American style. Houses were set back far from the street, in the center of large, tree-shaded grounds. Architectural historian James Marston Fitch called this "an attractive hybrid, a kind of Philadelphia suburb in the tropics." Not many years later, this Garden District would give birth to another hybrid of styles and arts, a creation whose luminosity in Carnival was never surpassed.

From 1841 to 1844, processions of the Bedouins were mounted sporadically, and without prior announcement. In 1845, the parade failed to appear at all, and the Creole press began to write of Mardi Gras as a memory. This observation from *L'Abeille* offers rich insight into the Creole perspective:

> Thousands of persons who yesterday had located themselves in the windows, balconies, and upon the sidewalks of the different streets through which the procession of masquers usually pass, were sadly disappointed in the non-appearance. This long established custom, which in the palmy days of the Ancien Regime was wont to be celebrated with grotesque pageantry . . . has, within the last few years, been gradually falling into disuse, not the less so from the abandonment of the old master spirits who led on the merry crowd, than from the lewd and miserable crew, who, of late years have been permitted to join in the celebration. It is a custom, however, "more honored in the breach than in observance," and we hope it will be henceforth regarded with "the things that were."

During the closing years of the 1840s and the early 1850s Mardi Gras was plagued by foul weather and reckless mischief. Boys had tossed flour in the streets for many years on unsuspecting maskers, on one another, and on those unmasked and wearing their everyday clothes. When the flour was replaced by quicklime, dust, and an occasional brick, there were numerous injuries. Each year brought fewer maskers to the streets, and by the midcentury, both Creole and American papers lamented the death of Mardi Gras.

The *Daily Delta* in 1851 commented:

> We can remember when the processions used to extend several squares, and embraced a great multitude and variety of oddities, all duly marshaled and commanded. But alas! the world grows everyday more practical, less sportive and imaginative—and more indifferent to the customs and institutions of the past. Mardi Gras, with all its laughter-moving tomfooleries, must go the way of all our other institutions, and reposing on its past glory, may content itself with sneering at the hard realities of the present locomotive, telegraphic age.

Creole masquerades and private entertainments continued, but the continuing onslaught of flour and lime marked the end of public festivities. In his landmark Carnival history, *The Mistick Krewe*, Perry Young described the cultural alchemy that was about to take place: "1856 was the last year that the Creoles could call Mardi Gras peculiarly their own. Their press had disclaimed it, and in the following year the Saxons assumed leadership and, with organization, persistence, and good weather, brought the festival to a degree of perfection which the Creole soon acknowledged with pride, and in which his spirit and genius have remained predominant."

Mardi Gras morning of 1857 was calm and relatively free of festivities, but evening brought crowds and carriage loads of revelers to the streets, many of them to satisfy the curiosity stirred by press reports of a mysterious new parade and the Mistick Krewe of Comus. Though the sky was studded with stars, the uptown streets were in darkness. "Suddenly, as if by magic, music sounded, torches were ablaze, and the whole assembly, Krewe and all, seemed to have emerged from the bowels of the earth." Amid a marching horde of masked and costumed devils rolled the first two floats of scenic pageantry in New Orleans. Preceded by brass bands and surrounded by a ring of torches, the first float carried the masked god, Comus, greeting spectators with his golden cup. The second car carried Satan, "high on a hill, far blazing as a mount, with pyramids and towers from diamond quarries hewn, and rocks of gold, the palace of great Lucifer."

New Orleans, with her passions for theater and parades, was stunned. This first torch-lit procession of the Mistick Krewe of Comus was hailed as "a revolution in street pageantry, a revelation in artistic effects." Comus introduced spectacle to the streets of New Orleans, and Carnival was forever changed. Comus would not only reappear every Mardi Gras night; he would do so amid the flames and smoking flares of moving theater, and each year he would present new visions to astonish a population long nourished on masquerades, parades, and stagecraft. With the advent of the Mistick Krewe of Comus, the festivities of Mardi Gras were closed with public pomp—with mystery, artistry, and ritual splendor.

Comus paraded for five years, from 1857 to 1861, with a series of triumphs that included "The Classic Pantheon" (1858), "The English Holidays" (1859), and "The Four Ages of Life" (1861). During the Civil War, Mardi Gras was not celebrated, and beginning in 1862 Comus did not appear for four years. In 1866, only days before Mardi Gras, the press announced that Comus would return "with his sacred mysteries." In those tumultuous years of war, followed by the ongoing military occupation of Reconstruction, New Orleans began her adjustment to reduced circumstances of wealth and position. It was during this period that Carnival ceased to be merely a beloved festival, and became a counter-kingdom, an otherworldly empire in which the worldly old city still reigned.

The year 1870 brought the first appearance of the Twelfth Night Revelers and the beginning of the Golden Age of Mardi Gras: Rex, king of Carnival, made his first appearance in 1872, and was soon followed by the Knights of Momus (1872), the Phunny Phorty Phellows (1878), and the Krewe of Proteus (1882). From 1870 until the onset of the Great Depression in 1930, this Golden Age of Mardi Gras counted hundreds of pageants with thousands of the shimmering papier-mâché apparitions known as floats. Those fabulous images and the artists who created them are the subjects of this book.

Comus, Rex, Momus, and Proteus are names long familiar and beloved in New Orleans, and several histories of these venerable and highly secretive old-line krewes have been compiled. Their lavish balls could be attended only by those fortunate enough to have received invitations, but their processions of floats, lights, and music could be viewed by anyone who cared to, and vast crowds lined the city's streets. What they saw during this Golden Age was ebullient public art of the highest rank, a series of displays acclaimed then as the finest, most brilliant in the world. The artists and builders who created those fabled pageants have remained obscure or unknown, their amazing body of work largely forgotten. The surviving watercolor float plates and the chromolithographed Carnival Bulletins (which were also known as Carnival Editions) at first impress one as finely rendered illustrations, and many of them invoke comparisons to the work of artists such as Tenniel, Granville, or Wyeth. These Mardi Gras masterworks, however, were not illustrations—they were designs for the rolling theatrical architecture of the evanescent pageants, and there is ample evidence they were built and decorated with great accuracy and attention to detail.

The float chassis were wooden caissons and wagons with steel-rimmed wooden wheels; at the front of each float were two chains that hooked into the harnesses of mule teams. The animals were caparisoned from head to hoof in white robes, as horses had been dressed in the days of chivalry, and they were led by robed and cowled attendants. The floats were drawn at perfect pace for phantom cargo, moving through streets paved with large stones that once had served as ballast. Richly costumed krewe members, their faces hidden behind hollow-eyed masks, rode on the float stage decks; above them rose temples, castles, bowers, clouds, flames, or waves—whatever the subject demanded, all made of papier-mâché, lavishly decorated, and touched with swirls of gold and silver leaf. As the floats rolled, everything on them swayed and quivered with otherworldly grace and strangeness; they would *appear*, emerging through glowing fogs that billowed from acrid, smoking calcium flares. The incomparable lights were reflected from polished, rectangular metal plates atop torches called "flambeaux," which were borne aloft by bands of robed and hooded Negroes—these ceremonial fires ringed every float, bathing them in clouds of intoxicating, pulsing magic.

The processions of Carnival were belated messengers of the baroque world, where order in the secular realm and ecstasies of the religious were revealed in theaters of spectacle, pageantry, and pyrotechnics. The architecture of the floats, like baroque palaces and altars, overwhelmed the viewer with wonder, to which was added a panoply of glorious effects they alone could summon. To revel in their trappings was to abandon one's sense of self, time, or place—to experience the transforming power of art in a festive exaltation of the senses.

Bror Anders Wikstrom, "Rex, No. 1 Car," chromolithograph of float design for Rex pageant, 1910: "The Freaks of Fable."

MARDI GRAS TREASURES

FLOAT DESIGNS OF THE GOLDEN AGE

Charles Briton, "Iguana," watercolor design for papier-mâché walking figure in Comus pageant, 1873: "The Missing Links to Darwin's Origin of Species."

CHAPTER I

CHARLES BRITON

The earliest surviving design for the New Orleans Carnival is a preliminary watercolor sketch for "Flora Drawn by Butterflies," float number four in the Comus pageant of 1858, "The Classic Pantheon." This anonymous work and a later engraving of the parade, which first appeared in the *London Illustrated News,* are the only visual remnants of the Comus productions before the Civil War. The album of designs for "Triumph of Epicurus" (Comus, 1867) was in the possession of a private library in 1930, but has since disappeared. An engraving of the "Epicurus" parade for *Harper's Magazine,* which pictured the Mistick Krewe marching as the courses of a monumental papier-mâché feast, remains our only visual record of the years between the end of the war and the early work of Charles Briton.

Briton, a native of Gothenburg, Sweden, arrived in New Orleans around 1865, following his adventures with Maximilian's army in Mexico. The young Swede, then in his midtwenties, was soon employed by lithographer Emile Boehler, and resided with the Boehler family for ten years at 456 Bienville Street in the French Quarter. Briton was stricken with yellow fever in 1868 and nearly died, but he was nursed back to health by the Boehlers. The following year brought Briton's earliest known Carnival design, the ensemble tableau for the Comus Ball of 1870, "Louisiana: Her Founders and Defenders."

The reign of the carpetbagger had begun in Louisiana, and several exceptional parades during the era of Reconstruction, all of them designed by Briton, took expert comic aim at the governing powers. The Carnival season of 1871 was opened on the evening of January 6 by the Twelfth Night Revelers with the pageant "Mother Goose's Tea Party." The political satire of this procession is lost to us today, but some of its malevolent wit lingers in the caricatures. *Jewell's Crescent City* pointed out that the Mother Goose rhymes "were written by one of the most popular members of the New Orleans press," a reference to E. C. Hancock, a prominent newspaper editor and native of Pennsylvania.

When the Louisiana election of 1872 resulted in two governors and two rival legislatures each claiming victory, the Radical Republican board of returns sided with William Pitt Kellogg, the Vermont-born carpetbagger. Federal troops were already stationed throughout New Orleans for months, and on the morning of January 6, three more companies of soldiers arrived to support Kellogg. That evening, the Twelfth Night Revelers delighted spectators with their torch-lit procession, "The World of Audubon."

The Audubon production, an apparent tribute to the great naturalist and former New Orleans resident, was also counted years later as among the finest of all Carnival creations, by virtue of its costumes. The Parrot, Pelican, Ibis, Flamingo, Owl, Cardinal, Vulture, and others were all wrought in endless layers of Parisian silks and velvets; but to the observing eye, they were only part of a greater feast. Among the seventeen floats were: "Political Barnyard Meeting," with Fox addressing Fowls; "The Crows in Council," depicting the Louisiana state legislature as Ravens and Crows of all kinds, the Carrion Crow with carpetbag in hand; the last float was "The Pelican," the insignia of the state of Louisiana, feeding her three fledglings, who kept falling from the nest. The pageant was followed by a tableau ball at the New Opera House. Charles Briton's watercolor of the ensemble tableau is the only visual remnant of the evening.

Seven weeks later, the Mistick Krewe of Comus closed the season with Carnival's satirical masterpiece, "The Missing Links to Darwin's Origin of Species." The Missing Links were the characters in a brilliantly layered satire; the pageant presented itself as a travesty of Darwin's theory, then regarded as an abomination by many. The order of march followed the stanzas of a masterful poem by Hancock—each stanza was borne aloft on transparencies (forms of glass, illuminated from within), in a succession of verse that identified each group and traced the evolution of life from Sponge to Gorilla. The Mistick Krewe were all on foot, inside 100 wondrous papier-mâché animals, fish, flowers, insects, and sea creatures, some of them twelve feet high; and in the glare of torches, the political targets of the Comus satire were revealed, in costumes as capricious as wanton nature's germ.

Many of the links bore unmistakable resemblances to political figures of the day, from local precincts to the White House: the Bloodhound was Badger, superintendent of the Metropolitan Police; the Rattlesnake was former governor Warmoth; Snail and Leech were members of the Louisiana

legislature; the Hyena stooped with booty was General "Beast" Butler; and Tobacco Grub wore the face of Pres. Ulysses S. Grant. Speculation about the "Missing Links" author may not have been intense to the public, but recent scholarship suggests that it lingered some time after the parade. Three months later, E. C. Hancock was attacked late at night on the street by a group of Metropolitan Police, beaten with savagery described as an assassination attempt. Following his recovery, this descendant of John Hancock left his adopted home and moved to New York City, where he continued his successful career in journalism.

Briton's remarkable designs for "The Missing Links," unseen and unknown in 1873, were rescued from oblivion in 1931 when two dozen of the plates appeared in Perry Young's *Mistick Krewe*. Throughout Carnival's Golden Age, everything connected with the design, housing, or construction of the pageants was secret and hidden. No one was to know how these hieratic visions came to be—they "were." To the krewe captains and design committees, however, the anonymous Briton became quite well known, for all of the early Carnival societies turned to him to design every aspect of their productions—floats, costumes, tableau ball settings, and invitations.

The tableaux cars introduced by the Mistick Krewe of Comus were not always used in subsequent pageants; for all of their innovative significance, they remained a theatrical device—one that was employed some years, but not others. Comus parades had no given format: in some years the Mistick Krewe marched on foot, inside large papier-mâché forms, as they did in "Four Ages of Life" (1861) and "Triumph of Epicurus" (1867). The "Lalla Rookh" production (1868), however, was a cavalcade; "The Missing Links" was the last major procession on foot. The marching and dancing casts of these parades could not be seen beyond the first or second row of spectators, and the Comus spectacle for 1874, "The Visit of Envoys from the Old World and New to the Court of Comus," was the first composed exclusively of floats.

Briton's agility with caricature, his taste for the comically grotesque, and his flare for satirical tableaux were central to many of the parades of the late 1870s and early 1880s. In 1877, during the waning days of Reconstruction, the Knights of Momus presented "Hades, a Dream of Momus," the most vitriolic parade in Carnival history. The powers on the Potomac and their scalawag allies were depicted as Satan, Beelzebub, and Moloch, with their retinues of lackeys, devils, and demons; official Washington was outraged.

Rex pageants of this period were also humorous and lighthearted. In 1878 the Briton designs poked fun at a range of political and social institutions, including fashion, abstinence, and lawyers. If anyone missed the visual jests, they could always read the write-ups in the press, and in the special Carnival Editions that were beginning to appear. These were souvenir papers of each parade with drawings and explanatory descriptions of the floats, such as this description for "The Supreme Court of Hell": "As we are told that lawyers are unknown in heaven, and as we know no greater punishment than to be constantly engaged in litigation . . ."

Briton moved effortlessly from popular travesty to classic myth, and his designs were drawn from themes that became the favored realms of the krewes—mythology, epic literature, history, and fancy. The Momus pageant "A Dream of Fair Women" (1880) and Rex's delightful "Pursuit of Pleasure" (1882) marked their departures from comic themes—and from unadorned scenic cars. In 1882 Momus presented "The Ramayama," with sixteen floats illustrating scenes such as "The Temple of Indra," "The Council of the Gods," and "Sita's Descent into the Earth." The Rex subject for 1883 was "Atlantis—The Antediluvian World," with depictions of "The Temple of Poseidon," "Hanging Gardens of Atlantis," and "Sacrifice Before the Column of Orickalaun."

With the exception of the satirical last float in the Comus parade of 1877 ("Our Future Destiny—1976," which depicted women voting and men housekeeping), the Mistick Krewe continued in its selection of lofty themes: "Spenser's 'Faerie Queen'" (1871), "Dreams of Homer" (1872), "Scenes from the Metamorphoses of Ovid" (1878), "The Myths of Northland" (1881), and "Worships of the World" (1882). Of the myriad design plates Briton created for these seminal Carnival productions, only two complete sets, those for "Mother Goose" and "The Missing Links," have survived. We are far more

fortunate with his work for the Krewe of Proteus: the first captain of Proteus, Judge George Theard, was also the earliest of Mardi Gras conservationists, and all of the float plates and many of the costume designs of his twenty-year tenure were preserved.

With the advent of Proteus in 1882, Carnival's Golden Age began to flower. Their inaugural pageant, "Ancient Egyptian Theology," was one of the era's most spectacular—an architectural display of papier-mâché temples, tombs, sacred animals, and resurrection. Proteus was the first krewe with a sizeable Creole membership and a Creole captain, and their Egyptian triumph was followed by "The History of France," with eighteen tableaux featuring ancient Druid gods, medieval churches, gothic castles, the discovery of Louisiana, and the execution of Marie Antoinette. In 1884, Proteus turned to the epic poem, *The Aeneid*, the designs for which would be Briton's last: the striking "Vestibule of Avernus," the fantastic architecture in "The Gate of Ivory" and "Palace of Pluto," and the fiery "Death of Dido."

Charles Briton died at the age of forty-four on the morning of July 1, 1884, while working in his office on Exchange Place. Apoplexy was recorded as the cause of death, but Briton had been in failing health. His young neighbor and fellow Swede, Bror Anders Wikstrom, had helped him to finish the designs for Rex, and Briton's will (which left savings of $4,000 to his godson, a member of the Boehler family) was written only three days before he died. The properties inventoried in his succession reveal him, the creator of countless fantasias and opulent décors, to have lived and worked in the minimally furnished rooms of an ascetic. Listed among his books, which included numerous histories, were *Shakespeare's Works*, *Don Quixote* (illustrated by Dore), Racinet's *Le Costume Historique*, *Natural History*, *The Races of Man*, Parton's *Caricature and Comic Art*, Manning's *Livestock Encyclopedia*, *The Arabian Nights*, and *Lettres de Mme. de Sevigne*. Also counted were "a lot of costume plates, and sketches, and lithographer's paper, known as Bristol Boards and cut into sheets, used by the deceased for sketches and plates, appraised together at the sum of twenty dollars." His brief obituary, published three weeks earlier, contained no mention of his Carnival work.

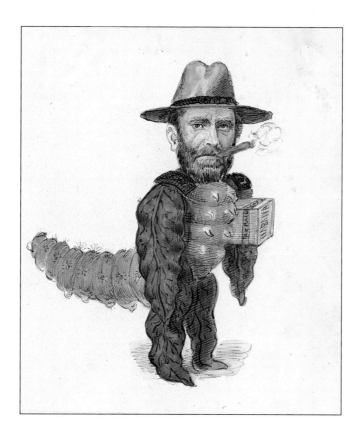

Above: *Charles Briton, "Tobacco Grub," watercolor design for papier-mâché walking
figure in Comus pageant, 1873: "The Missing Links to Darwin's Origin of Species."*

Below: *Charles Briton, "Old King Cole," watercolor float design for Twelfth Night
Revelers pageant, 1871: "Mother Goose's Tea Party."*

Above: *Charles Briton, "Hyena," watercolor design for papier-mâché walking figure in Comus pageant, 1873: "The Missing Links to Darwin's Origin of Species."*

Below: *Charles Briton, watercolor design for papier-mâché walking figures in
Twelfth Night Revelers pageant, 1871: "Mother Goose's Tea Party."*

"Nettle."

"Crab."

"Triton."

"Moth."

"Magnolia."

"Orang."

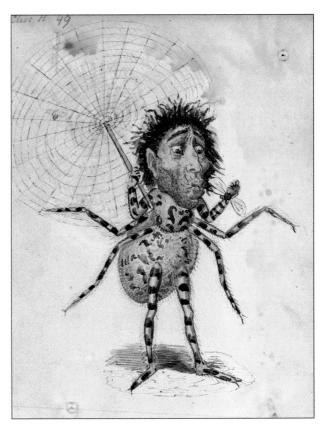

"Spider."

"Grape."

"Zebra."

Charles Briton, "New Orleans Carnival," lithograph for Rex edition, 1880.

Charles Briton, detail of lithograph of float designs for Momus pageant, 1877:
"Hades, a Dream of Momus."

Opposite, top: *Charles Briton, "Rapp, the Gnome King," watercolor float design for Momus pageant, 1878: "The Realms of Fancy."*

Opposite, bottom: *Charles Briton, "Summer and Winter Fairies," watercolor float design for Momus pageant, 1878: "The Realms of Fancy."*

Above: *Charles Briton, "A Midsummer Night's Dream," watercolor float design for Momus pageant, 1878: "The Realms of Fancy."*

Above: *Charles Briton, "Morte d'Arthur," watercolor float design for Momus pageant, 1878: "The Realms of Fancy."*

Opposite, top: *Charles Briton, "Ra," watercolor float design for Proteus pageant, 1882: "Ancient Egyptian Theology."*

Opposite, bottom: *Charles Briton, "Sacred Animals," watercolor float design for Proteus pageant, 1882: "Ancient Egyptian Theology."*

Opposite, top: *Charles Briton, "Innundation of the Nile," watercolor float design for Proteus pageant, 1882: "Ancient Egyptian Theology."*

Opposite, bottom: *Charles Briton, "Neith," watercolor float design for Proteus pageant, 1882: "Ancient Egyptian Theology."*

Above: *Charles Briton, "Title Car," watercolor float design for Proteus pageant, 1883: "The History of France."*

The Vestibule of Avernus.

Opposite, top: *Charles Briton, "Vestibule of Avernus," watercolor float design for Proteus pageant, 1884: "The Aeneid."*

Opposite, bottom: *Charles Briton, "Death of Dido," watercolor float design for Proteus pageant, 1884: "The Aeneid."*

Above: *Charles Briton, "Palace of Pluto," watercolor float design for Proteus pageant, 1884: "The Aeneid."*

Charles Briton, "The Gate of Ivory," watercolor float design for Proteus pageant,
1884: "The Aeneid."

CHAPTER II

CARLOTTA BONNECAZE

arlotta Bonnecaze made her astonishing debut as a Carnival designer with the Proteus procession of 1885, "Myths and Worships of the Chinese." The descriptions that appeared in the *Times-Democrat* newspaper and in the lithographed Carnival Bulletin were written by Lafcadio Hearn: "Proteus appears in the guise of Tien-Dze, Sun of Heaven. He wears the yellow imperial costume, and is bestriding the Fong-Hoang, or Phoenix of the Chinese, upon the summit of Mount Vou-Vai, that is the mountain of crystal, gold, silver and precious stones, containing everything, and yet out of which there is nothing."

Next came one of Carnival's sublime tableaux, "Creation," with its ingenious use of gauze, a material not readily associated with float construction.

The second tableau represents Pouan-Kou, the Chinese first man, born of an egg, the shell of which is the firmament, the white the air, and the yolk the earth. Resting upon a black, confused mass, representing chaos, is an immense egg. The sun appears upon the upper portion of its broken shell, darting its rays upon the earth, represented by the yolk (which is seen through a gauze representing the air) and upon which Pouan-Kou stands in his quaint costume of leaves. The lower portion of the shell represents the heavens at night, with stars scintillating like so many diamonds.

There were lavish depictions of "The Birth of Confucius," festivals, mythic creatures, and ancestral halls. And then, through the haze of flambeaux glare, the pageant concluded with "Ti-Can, Judgment of the Dead," and with visions of heaven and hell. A majestic pavilion rose in the center of "Paradise," an ornamental garden of golden vines, bejeweled palms, and musical bells. "Giehva" offered two hells for the wicked, one a massive cavern composed of ice, the other, waves of flame.

Mystery surrounds the life of Carlotta Bonnecaze, the most elusive of Carnival artists, and the one most devoted to the fantastic. Preliminary pen and ink float sketches attributed to her long ago by the Louisiana State Museum are the only record that she ever existed. There is abundant information about the Bonnecaze family, but never a mention of our mysterious Carlotta. The man we suspect was her father, Alexis Bonnecaze, was a member of Proteus, and very active in French cultural activities; he was also the founder (and perhaps sole member) of a curious dramatic society. We were also told by a relative that the Carlotta Bonnecaze who died on Mardi Gras 1930 had been named for her great-aunt. It is perhaps fitting that this study of the Carnival artists should include such an enigmatic figure; her strange body of work should remain attributed to Carlotta, until scholarship can establish another name.

Bonnecaze was the first woman as well as the first Creole to design floats and costumes for a Carnival krewe. Theology and whimsy were her strongest subjects—"Myths and Worships of the Chinese" (1885), "Visions of Other Worlds" (1886), "The Hindoo Heavens" (1889), "Asgard and the Gods" (1895), and "Dumb Society" (1896). For twelve years Bonnecaze worked exclusively for Proteus, and the sea god's processions offered scenes of unique strangeness.

Bonnecaze's development of the Chinese theme and the detailed magnificence of her designs reflected inspiration and careful study. Her "Visions of Other Worlds," however, were rooted solely in her formidable imagination—golden salamanders holding high Carnival on the surface of "The Sun"; a bevy of scorched black-skinned, blonde-haired female denizens of "Mercury," seated beneath leafy umbrellas; deranged green and yellow cometmen zipping through space on a chunky "Comet"; and six-armed inhabitants of "Saturn," cavorting amid enormous golden cacti. In addition to its unusual theme, "Visions of Other Worlds" also marked the first appearance of Proteus on Mardi Gras night, which in 1886 fell on March 9, the latest date in the history of the festival.

Following the Comus pageant of 1884, "Illustrated Ireland," the Mistick Krewe withdrew from Carnival, and for six years staged neither parade nor ball. On Mardi Gras night of 1887, Proteus again closed the season, with eighteen tableaux illustrating "Andersen's Fairy Tales." The title placard was held in place by a towering papier-mâché bee, standing eighteen feet high. Eerie, half-formed lioness-like creatures, fashioned of earth, rose from the cavern floor of "The Magician's Den." Other tableaux included: "Inge and the Marsh Woman," "The Castle of Dreams," and "The Snow Queen's Palace."

Bonnecaze turned to the gods and goddesses of ancient India for the Proteus display of 1889, "The Hindoo Heavens." The sea god appeared as Narayana, "the source and refuge of beings, born on the waters, creator, preserver and destroyer of worlds," seated beneath an enormous white lotus. In his wake came a host of deities, among them gods of Sun, Moon, Ocean, Riches, and Wisdom. One float depicted the paradise of Brahma, another the paradise of Indra, and the pageant closed with a great white winged horse, "Kalki-Avatar."

A few months after this spectacle, Comus announced that he would appear on Mardi Gras of 1890, and he let it be known that he expected Proteus to return to his usual Monday night. Proteus, however, regarded this current incarnation of Comus as a new one, with no title to the legacy of the first Mistick Krewe. This battle of Carnival gods unfolded like one of the many spirited contests of Greek mythology, where the old deities vied with one another, and with mankind, in pursuit of love or golden apples. The Mardi Gras struggle brought the era's sense of empire to theatrical life— for the first and only time in Carnival history, two rival krewes paraded simultaneously on Canal Street, Comus with "Palingenesis of the Mistick Krewe," Proteus with "Elfland." When the two pageants converged at Bourbon Street, Comus prevailed. In the year that followed his "Palingenesis," Comus chose "Demonology" as his subject; Proteus also paraded on Mardi Gras night, with "Tales of the Genii," and without incident, and the next year returned to his original Monday evening.

The Arabian fantasies of "The Genii" were followed by some of Bonnecaze's most beautifully painted designs, "A Dream of the Vegetable Kingdom." The subtle layers of her colors in "Ferns" and "Sea Plants" may have disappeared in the smoke and glare of parade lights, but the charm and humor of "Green Peas" linger. Seated inside an enormous pod were five plump young Peas, their human faces masks of dread and consternation as they fended off the attack of three huge caterpillars.

In 1893, the subject was "Kalevala," myths of Finland, which included: "The Rival Minstrels, Wainamoinen and Youkahainen," "Aarni and Mammelainen, Guardians of the Treasure," "Terhenstar, Daughter of the Fog," and "Taehti, the Polar Star." The Persian epic of kings, "Shah Nameh," unfolded in the tableaux of 1894, with "Tahumers, the Binder of Demons," "Rustum and the Dragon," "The Ordeal by Fire," and "The Tree of Wisdom," and closed with a Bonnecaze leitmotif, "Zerdusht's Vision of Heaven." For his following pageant, Proteus once again drew upon a northern pantheon, "Asgard and the Gods." Among the scenes depicted were: "Gilling and the Black Dwarfs," "Muspelheim, the Home of Brightness," "Loki in Chains," and "Ogir, the Ocean God."

The Golden Age of Carnival artistry reached its zenith in the closing years of the Belle Epoque. One season, that of 1896, glowed brightest, by virtue of two unsurpassed productions, the Momus Ball, "A Comic History of Rome," with its miniature pageant of papier-mâché floats on the stage of the French Opera House, and the Proteus parade of Bonnecaze designs, "Dumb Society." Anthropomorphic images were familiar devices in the masks, costumes, and tableaux of Carnival, and whimsy was no stranger. What set "Dumb Society" apart, what placed it among Carnival's greatest works, was the sly charm, the perfectly pitched wit of Bonnecaze's gorgeous watercolors.

Each of "Dumb Society's" eighteen scenes was set amid the papier-mâché décors of nature, and featured various members of the animal kingdom, all clothed in human costumes and performing human activities. "In Court" presented Fox as the defendant, Hen as her accuser; Owl was the judge and Goose the clerk; the emblem of law in this woodland setting was a jackass bust of gold. "The Upper Crust" offered a parade of peacocks, with the homeliest of the peahens holding a mirror, in which she might admire her snooty beauty. Lion presided at the table of "A Royal Banquet," a gentle travesty of after-dinner speeches; Parrots, Turtles, and Cockatoo danced amid the blazing palmettos of "At Home—Dancing"; White Mice primped and pranced in their organdy pinafores, beneath the steady gazes of "Watchful Guardians," papier-mâché cats standing eighteen feet high; and in "Last Rites," a collection of avian and insect mourners prepared to bury Cock Robin.

The Bonnecaze tableaux for "Dumb Society" were neither fables nor satires. There were no morals to be drawn and their occasional barbs (the homely peahens of "The Upper Crust," the elephantine hostess of "Five O'Clock Tea") were more like jests, direct but not cutting, and tempered with knowing, affectionate good humor. Indeed, much of the pageant's comedy was to be found in the fanciful costumes and delightful gestures of its cast: in the mobcapped Duckling clutching her baby-duck doll; in the Rat dressed in prison stripes toting a crowbar; in the bespectacled Flamingo fishing in his mackintosh; and in the elegantly liveried and beribboned Ass serving tea. More than a century after its creation, "Dumb Society" remains a one-of-a-kind masterpiece. It is the most inviting and appealing of family albums, a whimsical panorama of Creole domesticity and local social customs, of Belle Epoque manners and foibles, illuminated by the glorious imagination of the lost member of one of those large Creole families whose Golden Age, even then, was drawing to a close.

Above: Carlotta Bonnecaze, "Creation," watercolor float design for Proteus pageant, 1885: "Myths and Worships of the Chinese."

Opposite, top: Carlotta Bonnecaze, "Ti-Can, Judgment of the Dead," watercolor float design for Proteus pageant, 1885: "Myths and Worships of the Chinese."

Opposite, bottom: Carlotta Bonnecaze, "Paradise," preliminary pencil drawing for Proteus pageant, 1885: "Myths and Worships of the Chinese."

Pages 38-39: Carlotta Bonnecaze, "Paradise," watercolor float design for Proteus pageant, 1885: "Myths and Worships of the Chinese."

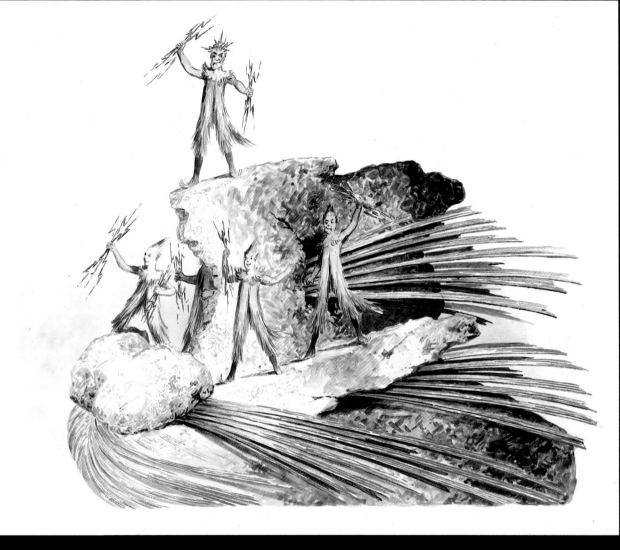

Opposite, top: Carlotta Bonnecaze, "Mercury," preliminary pencil drawing
for Proteus pageant, 1886: "Visions of Other Worlds."

Opposite, bottom: Carlotta Bonnecaze, "Mercury," watercolor float design
for Proteus pageant, 1886: "Visions of Other Worlds."

Above: Carlotta Bonnecaze, "Comet," watercolor float design for Proteus
pageant, 1886: "Visions of Other Worlds."

Opposite, top: *Carlotta Bonnecaze, "Title Car," watercolor float design for Proteus pageant, 1887: "Andersen's Fairy Tales."*

Opposite, bottom: *Carlotta Bonnecaze, "The Magician's Den," watercolor float design for Proteus pageant, 1887: "Andersen's Fairy Tales."*

Above: *Carlotta Bonnecaze, "The Castle of Dreams," watercolor float design for Proteus pageant, 1887: "Andersen's Fairy Tales."*

Carlotta Bonnecaze, "Proteus, No. 1 Car," watercolor float design for Proteus
pageant, 1889: "The Hindoo Heavens."

Carlotta Bonnecaze, "Surya, God of the Sun," watercolor float design for Proteus

Opposite, top: *Carlotta Bonnecaze, "The Good Genii," watercolor float design for Proteus pageant, 1891: "Tales of the Genii."*

Opposite, bottom: *Carlotta Bonnecaze, "The Enchanter," watercolor float design for Proteus pageant, 1891: "Tales of the Genii."*

Above: *Carlotta Bonnecaze, "Elves of Malaria," watercolor float design for Proteus pageant, 1890: "Elfland."*

Above: *Carlotta Bonnecaze, "Green Peas," watercolor float design for Proteus pageant, 1892: "A Dream of the Vegetable Kingdom."*

Opposite, top: *Carlotta Bonnecaze, "Sea Plants," watercolor float design for Proteus pageant, 1892: "A Dream of the Vegetable Kingdom."*

Opposite, bottom: *Carlotta Bonnecaze, "Ferns," watercolor float design for Proteus pageant, 1892: "A Dream of the Vegetable Kingdom."*

Opposite, top: *Carlotta Bonnecaze, "The Upper Crust," watercolor float design for Proteus pageant, 1896: "Dumb Society."*

Opposite, bottom: *Carlotta Bonnecaze, "Five O'Clock Tea," preliminary pencil drawing for Proteus pageant, 1896: "Dumb Society."*

Above: *Carlotta Bonnecaze, "Five O'Clock Tea," watercolor float design for Proteus pageant, 1896: "Dumb Society."*

Opposite, top: *Carlotta Bonnecaze, "A Royal Banquet," watercolor float design for Proteus pageant, 1896: "Dumb Society."*

Opposite, bottom: *Carlotta Bonnecaze, "Watchful Guardians," watercolor float design for Proteus pageant, 1896: "Dumb Society."*

Above: *Carlotta Bonnecaze, "At Spanish Fort," watercolor float design for Proteus pageant, 1896: "Dumb Society."*

Carlotta Bonnecaze, "Last Rites," watercolor float design for Proteus pageant,
1896: "Dumb Society."

CHAPTER III

BROR ANDERS WIKSTROM

The economic heights New Orleans enjoyed from 1850 to 1862 were never regained, but for another hundred years New Orleans remained the largest and wealthiest city in the South—and a magnet for artists. Portrait and landscape painters had always been in demand, while the city's numerous theaters and operas employed sculptors, scenic painters, and decorators, many of whom also worked in the secret preparations of Carnival's papier-mâché pageants and balls. Most large American cities presented similar prospects for artists, but New Orleans offered what many artists prized above opportunity—a daily life drenched in tropical light and sensual color, and a dreamlike cosmopolitan presence.

New Orleans was in the South, but not of the South. After sixty years of Americanization, New Orleans remained closer in culture and manner to Havana or Port au Prince than to any city in Georgia or Virginia. During the 1870s and early 1880s, the old city—the Creole sector—was already in decline, for many of its residents had left for the suburbs near Bayou St. John, and others had moved uptown. The St. Louis Hotel, once the grandest in the country and home of princely Creole revels, had also served as home to the radical Louisiana legislature, who left it a near ruin. Magnificent Creole mansions then in decay were being subdivided into apartments and filled with newly arrived Sicilian immigrants; they were joined by a smaller but longer-lasting influx of artists and writers who came from all parts of America, and some from Europe, to work and paint in New Orleans. These young artists were fascinated by the palpable antiquity and faded grandeur of the old quarter, with its narrow streets and picturesque architecture—balconies masked with intricate patterns of cast iron, once-grand town houses, quaint Creole cottages, and hidden courtyards rich with palms, banana trees, and tropical blossoms.

In the fall of 1872, young Edgar Degas came to visit his brother René, who had married a New Orleans Creole, Estelle Musson, and resided on Esplanade Avenue. René Degas was a prominent member of the newly formed New Orleans Cotton Exchange, the setting for one of the painter's early important works. Lafcadio Hearn arrived in New Orleans in 1877 and worked as a journalist and writer for eleven years. He was captivated by the city's exotic culture and fabulous textures, and recorded his observations in hundreds of newspaper columns that were later collected and called *Fantastics*.

Bror Anders Wikstrom came to New Orleans in 1883, a well-educated and well-traveled young man of thirty-five. A native of Stora Lassana, Sweden, Wikstrom was raised on a large estate governed by his aged, patriarchal father. The young man preferred his musical studies to the rigors of a classical education, and when he was fourteen he ran away to sea and the adventures of travel. Several years later he returned to Sweden, and studied art at the Royal Academy of Art in Stockholm; after further studies in Paris, he resumed his travels, and following exploratory visits to New York, Florida, and Mexico, he moved to New Orleans.

Wikstrom became a member of all the local art movements, and a founder of the Art Association of New Orleans. His large apartment in the old sector also served as his studio, and he held regular open houses for fellow artists; years later they recalled his beautiful piano playing, and the Parisian style of his atelier, decorated with "hangings of armor, rugs, ornamented furniture, and all sorts of 'artist's properties.'" Among the artists Wikstrom met was his close neighbor and fellow Swede, Charles Briton. When Briton grew ill, Wikstrom worked as his assistant on the Carnival float and costume designs for 1884. Following his new friend's death, Wikstrom became the Rex designer, beginning an unbroken apostolic succession of Carnival artists.

The comic tone and frequent caricature of early Rex parades died with Briton. In a single decade Carnival floats had evolved tremendously, from small wagons and decorated platforms to elaborate papier-mâché creations; and Wikstrom's float designs mirrored the grandeur that Rex had begun to favor in 1883 with "Atlantis—The Antediluvian World." His palaces, kiosks, and follies were graced with starry arches and garlanded minarets; capitals and cornices were formed of spectral creatures; caverns and forests were floored with enormous crystals and gems. And leaves—leaves of every shape and color from nature and more from his imagination were painted with endless variation and flair. Rex himself was often enthroned in leafy bowers and regal canopies of papier-mâché leaves, as he was in 1893, "Fantasies"; in 1906, "In Utopia"; and in 1910, "The Freaks of Fable."

In contrast to Briton, whose name was unknown

to the public, Wikstrom was often referred to in print as the acknowledged dean of Carnival artists. He remained better known, however, for his marine paintings and occasional landscapes, and for his prominence in New Orleans art circles. He continued to travel and paint throughout Mexico, and after each Mardi Gras he would journey to Paris or Stockholm. But Wikstrom always returned to New Orleans, and the twenty-five years of his residence were a Golden Age in the arts.

Two other important members of Wikstrom's art circle were the Woodward Brothers, Ellsworth and William, who migrated to New Orleans from Massachusetts, and taught a range of subjects—drawing, painting, architecture, and pottery—at Tulane and Newcomb colleges. Their first exhibitions were mounted by the Art Association, which Wikstrom helped found in 1885, the year of their arrival. The Woodwards' impressionistic paintings and watercolors reveled in the intense color and sensual textures of the old Creole city and environs. William, the architect, was an early preservationist, and in 1895 successfully fought the proposed demolition of the Cabildo, the seat of colonial government. Wikstrom also taught at the Art Association, but it was through his long friendship with the Woodwards that the first Newcomb students and graduates began to assist him with his Carnival work.

Wikstrom designed the Rex parade for twenty-five years and the Proteus parade for ten years. For each of these pageants he created twenty watercolor float plates, approximately one hundred costume plates, and more for jewelry, masks, slippers, musical instruments, and paraphernalia. When one considers the vast number of these creations, it is maddening that only a single album of Rex float plates and several dozen Rex costume designs have survived; his Proteus work was fortunately preserved and is housed in the treasure vaults of Tulane University. The lithographed cartoons of the Carnival Bulletins thus became our only record of Wikstrom's watercolor Rex designs.

Among the Carnival designers, most of whom enjoyed other careers, only Wikstrom was a painter, and his love of painting, his elegant draftsmanship, and a recurring fondness for decorative neoclassical motifs distinguish his work. Wikstrom's earliest Rex designs illustrated floats that were grouped into parade divisions with curiously unrelated themes—in

1886, "The Triumph of Aurelian" and "Grand Historical Scenes"; in 1887, "Music and Drama," "Odds and Ends," and "Washington" (Mardi Gras that year fell on February 22, Washington's birthday).

On the eve of the Gilded Age of the 1890s, world-weary Europe and hormonal young America prepared themselves for the nineteenth century's coda, and for the march into a new century of progress and invention. New Orleans and Carnival, however, remained enraptured by the glories and splendors of the past, and the Rex pageant of 1889, "Treasures of the Earth," brought Wikstrom's first triumph. This glittering procession of precious ores and minerals was led by His Majesty, high atop his float decorated with the sculpted papier-mâché faces of masked revelers; indeed, every creature on this float, even the fanciful dragon supporting the royal canopy, was masked. In the pageants that followed, Wikstrom created a cornucopia of riches for the king of Carnival.

Perhaps in keeping with his motto, "Pro Bono Publico" (For the Public Good), Rex themes were more accessible than those of Comus—"Rulers of Ancient Times" (1890), "Symbolism of Colors" (1892), "Illustrations from Literature" (1894), "Heavenly Bodies" (1896), and "Harvest Queens" (1898). His Majesty bid a dreamy farewell to the 1800s with "Reveries of Rex," including floats such as "Isle of Delight," "Fantastic Refuge," and "Pavilion of the Gods." These visions rolled past scenes almost as strange as any float in the parade—the streets of New Orleans were covered with ice and snow.

Wikstrom's sorties into whimsy continued in "Terpsichore" (1900), with "The Frog Ballet" and "Sunset Dance of the Mosquito." His "Quotations from Literature" (1902) included the witty titles "The Prince of Darkness Is a Gentleman" and "Bacchus Has Drowned More Men than Neptune"; "Uneasy Lies the Head that Wears a Crown" depicted the twin dragons of nihilism and socialism gnawing at a castle's foundations. The Rex subject for 1906, "In Utopia," was a panorama of fanciful scenes, like "Where Aerial Navigation Is Perfect," with its strangely propelled creature-craft, and the zany underwater scene, "Where Submarines Are Used as Autos."

The Wikstrom designs for Proteus echoed his fascination with the East, and the watercolors selected for this book are heavily drawn from "Cleopatra" (1903) and "The Rubaiyat" (1905). Following the mute grandeur of the "Cleopatra" title car came some of Wikstrom's most glorious designs—the fantastically feathered chariot on "On the Way to Serapeum," the billowing silvered "Heavens," and the cabalistic illumination of "Isis Revealed." The "Rubaiyat" plates offered Wikstrom's most lyrical and intoxicating work: the sun-dappled horses and fiery chariot on "The Awakening"; the earthy sensuality pouring from "The Cup of Love"; the splendid "Glories of This World"; the dreamy, star-roofed cavern setting on "The Long Rest"; and the folds of starry veils presided over by "The Fates."

Proteus celebrated his Silver Anniversary in 1906 with "Inspirations of Proteus," including floats such as "Hindoo Mythology," "Persian Romance," and "Egyptian Myths." In the following year, Wikstrom again turned to *The Arabian Nights*, with the tale "The Queen of the Serpents" and its scenes of sacred scrolls, strange fruits, and crystal islands. "The Light of Asia" was the subject for 1908, with tableaux for "Love's Prison-House," "Kama, the King of Passions," and the "Lords of Light," seated inside hollowed celestial orbs amid streaming rays of light. Precious gems and jewelry, which had long been used as decorative float elements, became the subject matter for one of Wikstrom's finest efforts, the 1909 Rex production, "The Treasures of the King."

In the perpetual calendar of Carnival, Wikstrom had completed his designs for the 1910 pageants well before the Carnival of 1909. Shortly after Mardi Gras, Wikstrom, already ill, traveled to New York to design a procession of forty floats commemorating the discoveries of explorer Henry Hudson. During his two months in New York, he managed to complete the designs, but his health continued to deteriorate and he died there on April 26, 1909. Wikstrom's last parade for Rex, "The Freaks of Fable," rolled on Mardi Gras morning of 1910; towering above the title car was his testament, a winsome creature with jolly ruby eyes, whose head and body were entirely formed of layered leaves. When the New Orleans Museum of Art was erected in 1911, in the City Park whose palmettos he had painted, Wikstrom's name was carved into the stone of an exterior wall.

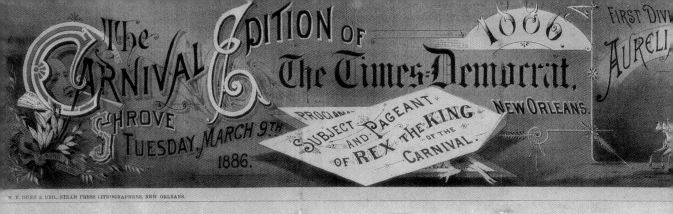

IUMPH.

Nº 1. GOLD AND TREASURES FROM ASIA. Nº 2. INDIAN RICHES.

Nº 6. ZENOBIA QUEEN OF PALMYRA. ROMAN MUSICIANS AND STANDARD BEARERS.

Nº 9. NOBLE LADIES OF ROME. Nº 10. GENIUS OF PEACE.

ANITY. Nº 14. ATTILA AT RAVENNA. Nº 15. THE FIRST FRENCH MONARCHIAL DYNASTY.

Nº 19. PETER THE HERMIT PREACHING THE FIRST CRUSADE. Nº 20. COLUMBUS' RETURN FROM HIS FIRST VOYAGE. Nº 21. LUTHER AT THE DIET IN WORMS.

BJECT * "SYMBOLISM OF COLORS" *

Nº 1 REX COAT OF ARMS

Nº 2 THE KING OF THE CARNIVAL.

R - MARTYRDOM

Nº 6 PALE GREEN - BAPTISM.

Nº 7 PURPLE - JUSTICE

Nº 11 SCARLET - GLORY

Nº 12 GREEN - FAITH

Nº 13 RED - CHARITY

Nº 17 ORANGE - MARRIAGE.

Nº 18 SILVER - CHASTITY

Nº 19 IRRIDESCENT

1893

CARNIVAL EDITION OF THE PICAYUNE

FEBRUARY 14th

REX

NEW ORLEANS

BOEUF GRAS.

Nº 4 GAMBOLS ON THE DEEP.

Nº 5 PASTIME IN HADES.

Nº 9 FAIRIES COURT.

Nº 10. SUN LAND.

Nº 11 HOME OF BRIGHTNESS

Nº 15. ON THE WAVES OF JOY.

Nº 16. SPORTS OF THE FAIRIES.

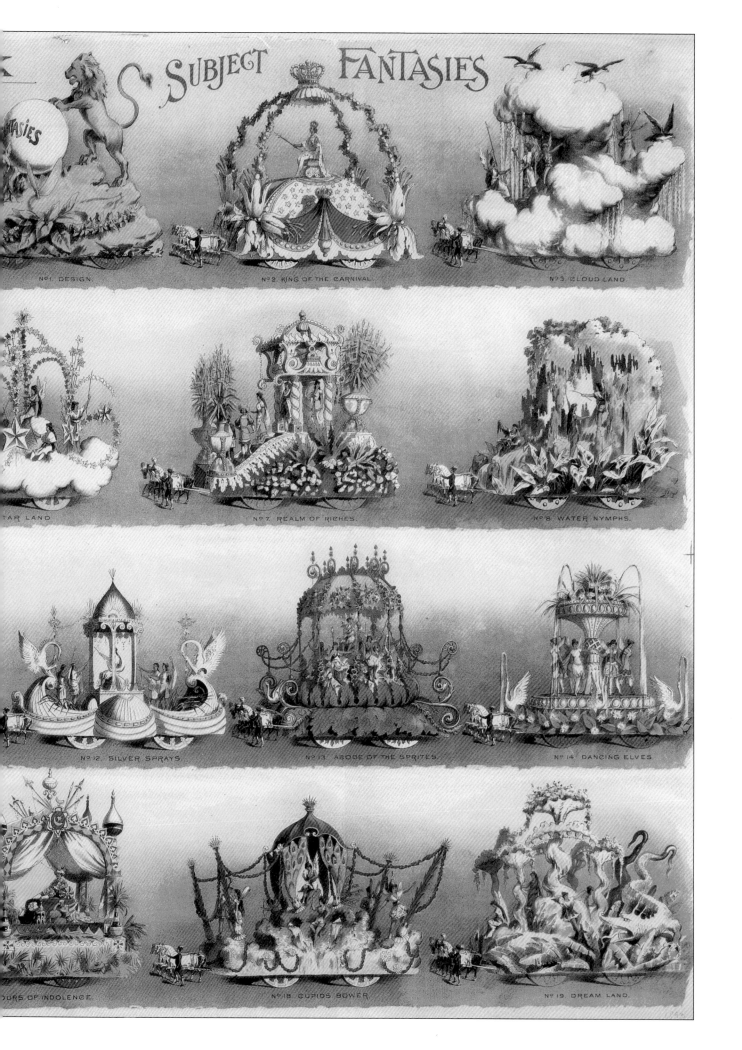

SUBJECT FANTASIES

Nº 1. DESIGN.　　Nº 2. KING OF THE CARNIVAL.　　Nº 3. CLOUD LAND.

TAR LAND.　　Nº 7. REALM OF RICHES.　　Nº 8. WATER NYMPHS.

Nº 12. SILVER SPRAYS.　　Nº 13. ABODE OF THE SPRITES.　　Nº 14. DANCING ELVES.

URS OF INDOLENCE.　　Nº 18. CUPIDS BOWER.　　Nº 19. DREAM LAND.

Pages 58-59: Bror Anders Wikstrom, "Triumph of Aurelian and Grand Historical Scenes," Carnival Edition of the Rex pageant, 1886. Chromolithography by M. F. Dunn, New Orleans.

Pages 60-61: Bror Anders Wikstrom, "Symbolism of Colors," Carnival Edition of the Rex pageant, 1892. Chromolithography by Daniel Anton Buechner.

Pages 62-63: Bror Anders Wikstrom, "Fantasies," Carnival Edition of the Rex pageant, 1893. Chromolithography by Daniel Anton Buechner.

Above: Bror Anders Wikstrom, "Title Car," watercolor float design for Proteus pageant, 1903: "Cleopatra."

Opposite, top: Bror Anders Wikstrom, "The Heavens," watercolor float design for Proteus pageant, 1903: "Cleopatra."

Opposite, bottom: Bror Anders Wikstrom, "Reign of the Gods on Earth," watercolor float design for Proteus pageant, 1903: "Cleopatra."

Opposite, top: Bror Anders Wikstrom, "Isis Revealed," watercolor float design for Proteus pageant, 1903: "Cleopatra."

Opposite, bottom: Bror Anders Wikstrom, "On the Way to Serapeum," watercolor float design for Proteus pageant, 1903: "Cleopatra."

Above: Bror Anders Wikstrom, "P—Proteus," watercolor float design for Proteus pageant, 1904: "The Alphabet."

Opposite, top: *Bror Anders Wikstrom, "U—Unicorn," watercolor float design for Proteus pageant, 1904: "The Alphabet."*

Opposite, bottom: *Bror Anders Wikstrom, "XYZ—The End," watercolor float design for Proteus pageant, 1904: "The Alphabet."*

Above: *Bror Anders Wikstrom, "Title Car," watercolor float design for Proteus pageant, 1905: "The Rubaiyat."*

Opposite, top: *Bror Anders Wikstrom, "The Awakening," watercolor float design for Proteus pageant, 1905: "The Rubaiyat."*

Opposite, bottom: *Bror Anders Wikstrom, "Glories of This World," watercolor float design for Proteus pageant, 1905: "The Rubaiyat."*

Above: *Bror Anders Wikstrom, "The Long Rest," watercolor float design for Proteus pageant, 1905: "The Rubaiyat."*

Opposite, top: *Bror Anders Wikstrom, "The Cup of Love," watercolor float design for Proteus pageant, 1905: "The Rubaiyat."*

Opposite, bottom: *Bror Anders Wikstrom, "Jamshyd," watercolor float design for Proteus pageant, 1905: "The Rubaiyat."*

Above: *Bror Anders Wikstrom, "The Fates," watercolor float design for Proteus pageant, 1905: "The Rubaiyat."*

Opposite, top: *Bror Anders Wikstrom, "Parwin and Mushtari," watercolor float design for Proteus pageant, 1905: "The Rubaiyat."*

Opposite, bottom: *Bror Anders Wikstrom, "The Recording Angel," watercolor float design for Proteus pageant, 1905: "The Rubaiyat."*

Above: *Bror Anders Wikstrom, "Youth and Age," watercolor float design for Proteus pageant, 1905: "The Rubaiyat."*

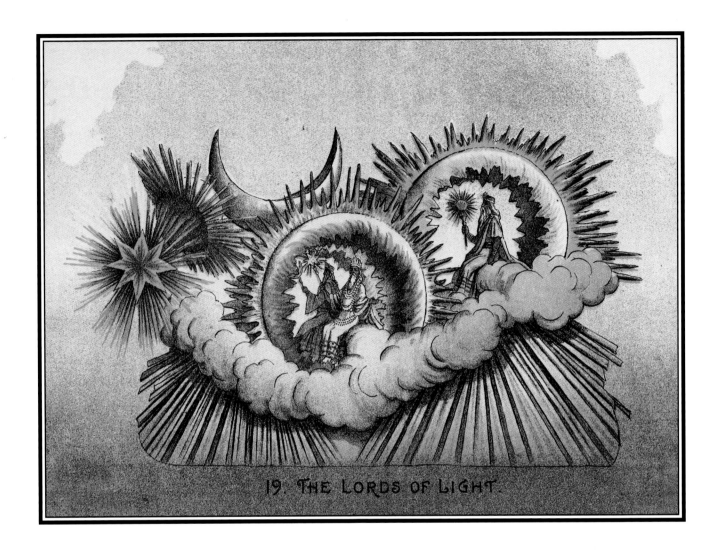

19. THE LORDS OF LIGHT.

Above: *Bror Anders Wikstrom, "The Lords of Light," chromolithograph of float design for Proteus pageant, 1908: "The Light of Asia."*

Opposite, top: *Bror Anders Wikstrom, "The Hydra," chromolithograph of float design for Rex pageant, 1910: "The Freaks of Fable."*

Opposite, bottom: *Bror Anders Wikstrom, "Where Submarines Are Used as Autos," chromolithograph of float design for Rex pageant, 1906: "In Utopia."*

CHAPTER IV

JENNIE WILDE

The Golden Age of Carnival saw a friendly rivalry among the krewes to mount the season's most memorable parade. Momus opened the festivities on his Thursday night, and Proteus appeared on the Monday evening before Mardi Gras. On Mardi Gras morning, Rex rolled with the only pageant that was bathed in sunlight, not the glare of torches. And with nightfall, when law decreed an end to masking, a final crowd of weary troupes reconvened, as they had since 1857, to await the appearance of Comus and his Mistick Krewe. Arthur Burton LaCour wrote in *New Orleans Masquerade*:

> Comus is more than a gathering of gentlemen on pleasure bent—he is mysticism, symbolism, poetry, and romance. Cloaked in secrecy and surrounded with the aura of the unknown, to reveal his working and tell of his following would, like tearing away the veil of the temple, destroy the illusion. So the Mistick Krewe of Comus parades down the years—fabulous, mysterious, inscrutable—the very soul of Carnival.

Lifting his enchanter's cup in greeting and farewell, Comus personified the power of the mask and the transitory glory of Carnival's fantastic empire. The last float of Comus was the last float of Carnival, and as it disappeared into the glowing fog it had created, the audience was reminded that dull reality and ashes would soon again be theirs.

Among the hundreds of extant designs for this glorious armada of dreams, the most ravishing examples of Carnival's extravagant, over-the-top aesthetic are found in the mature work of Virginia Wilkinson Wilde. Miss Jennie Wilde, as she was known throughout her career, was not a particularly gifted draftsman; even in her best work, the human figures remained stiff, the animals poorly drawn. The painting in Wilde's early float plates was likewise inauspicious, offering few of the pleasures found in the watercolors of her predecessor, Charles Briton, or those of her contemporaries, Carlotta Bonnecaze and Bror Anders Wikstrom. Yet, even then, Wilde's genius for design was established with a masterpiece, her first invitation for Comus in 1891, the coiled and striking green serpent of "Demonology." In the Comus float plates of her maturity lies the Rosetta stone of Carnival fabulosity.

Jennie Wilde was born on April 10, 1865, in Augusta, Georgia, into a distinguished Southern Irish Catholic family of jurists and writers. Her grandfather Richard Henry Wilde served as attorney general of Georgia, and was known as the author of the popular poem "My Life Is Like a Summer Rose." His scholarly two-volume work on the sixteenth-century Italian poet Torquato Tasso was published in 1842. In the following year he settled in New Orleans, to practice law, and later filled the chair of Constitutional Law at the University of Louisiana.

His son, Richard Henry Wilde, Jr., was a lawyer with literary interests, but his poetry was never published. Richard Wilde and his wife, Virginia, left New Orleans during the Civil War occupation and moved to Augusta. The family returned around 1870 and resided on Coliseum Square. Among their friends and neighbors was the family of Grace King; years later the venerable New Orleans writer recalled her friendship with Jennie Wilde in *Memories of a Southern Woman of Letters*.

Wilde studied painting and antique drawing at the Art Students League of New York and remained a member all of her life. She also studied at the Southern Art Union, and her work was exhibited by the Art Association of New Orleans from 1889 to 1892. Like her father, brother, and grandfather, Jennie Wilde won a fleeting reputation as a poet. Wilde's poems appeared frequently in the pages of the *Times-Democrat* newspaper, and her book of poetry, *Why, and Other Poems* (published in New Orleans in 1888), was well received.

Wilde worked as an illustrator, taught at a number of local institutes, and also painted the interior murals of the Church of Notre Dame on Jackson Avenue. But it was her work as the designer for Comus that garnered her early and ongoing acclaim. When Momus reappeared in 1900, following a hiatus of eleven years, he also turned to Wilde. At a time when professional opportunities for women were rare, and Carnival remained shrouded in mandarin secrecy, Wilde not only succeeded professionally, her triumphs were reported by the press.

A tall, handsome woman at the age of twenty-five, Wilde made her debut as the Comus designer in 1891 with "Demonology." Comus appeared atop a swarm of papier-mâché butterflies, seated inside an enormous morning glory, a leitmotif Wilde

repeated beautifully for two decades—Comus greeting the multitudes in a bower of pansies, or laurels, or lotus, or lilies of the valley, Momus upon a mound of chrysanthemums or spider lilies. Comus, drawn by sacred storks, closed Mardi Gras of 1892 with "Nippon, the Land of the Rising Sun." A few days after Ash Wednesday, the *Picayune* reported this scene from the Comus Ball at the French Opera House:

> It is not generally known, as it deserves to be, that the artist who made the designs for the recent splendid pageant of the Mistick Krewe of Comus was Miss Jennie Wilde of this City. The lady was made the recipient of a special honor at the magnificent ball which followed the street display. The Captain conducted Miss Wilde under the beautiful umbrella, brilliant with electric lights, and there presented her with a jeweled necklace and his cloak, a rich affair of blue silk velvet shot with pearls and embroidered in gold, which he had worn during the parade and tableaux.

The Japanese motifs frequently incorporated into designs of the aesthetic movement traveled effortlessly, as did Wilde, to art nouveau. More than any other Carnival designer, Wilde embraced the new style, creating the most florid designs of an already gilded age. She made little use of large figures (dragons and an occasional Pegasus were exceptions); her floats were covered with flowers, stars, crescent moons, and flamelike clouds in a style of frenzied elegance peculiarly hers. And while the sensuous, flowing lines animating Wilde's designs reflected her ongoing devotion to art nouveau, the subjects she frequently chose revealed her passion for the painting and literature of the Symbolists and the Decadents—for the eerie creatures of Jan Toorop and the Babylonian apocalypse of Jean Rochegrosse, for the sensually tinted worlds of Gustave Flaubert and Théophile Gautier. Writing in *One of Cleopatra's Nights*, Gautier exclaimed, "Our world is very small beside the ancient world; our feasts are paltry affairs compared with the terrifying banquets of Roman patricians and Asiatic princes. With our petty habits, we find it hard to conceive of those enormous existences which made reality of all the strangest, boldest, most monstrously impossible inventions of the imagination."

The subject presented by Comus in 1893 was "Salammbo," Flaubert's extravagant, operatic novel set in ancient Carthage. Among the tableaux Wilde created were: "The Feast in the Garden of Hamilcar," "The Veil of Tanit," "Torturing the Barbarians," "Xarxas with Gisco's Head," and "Sacrifice to Moloch." More than a decade later, for the Momus pageant of 1905, Wilde chose her most daring subject, "Vathek, Ninth Caliph of the Abassides." William Beckford's Eastern fantasy was written in the early years of the nineteenth century, when he was the wealthiest man in England. All Britain was scandalized by the rampant sensuality and homoeroticism in *Vathek*, and howled its indignation at what was likely taking place behind the wall surrounding Beckford's grandiose abbey, Fonthill.

The richness and energy that characterize Wilde's best work appear only tentatively in surviving plates from the end of the nineteenth century. Her designs for Comus invitations during this time—the golden cup of 1898, the swirling indigo sky of 1899, the serpentine corona of 1900—were all more interesting than her float designs for those respective years, illustrating "Scenes from Shakespeare," "Josephus," and "Stories of the Golden Age." A scattered handful of watercolor plates for Comus pageants of the early 1900s have survived, augmented by more numerous collections of float tracings. And while these roughly colored tracings pale beside her finished watercolors, they document the flowering of Wilde's hallmark extravagance—"The Golden Crab" from "The Fairy Kingdom" (1902) and "The Shrine of Ishtar," "The Temple of Shamash," and "The River of Night" from "Izdubar" (1904).

Wilde's pen-and-ink watercolor fantasias exhibited little interest in the architecture or décors of any era or locale, however exotic. The past rarely served as her backdrop for historical tableaux, but rather as the point of departure—for her landscapes of gilded trees and fiery clouds, bowers of gigantic flora, and streams of molten gold. Wilde used gold more frequently than any other designer, and she

painted it beautifully. Comus led his 1903 production, "A Leaf from the Mahabarata," atop a sinewy thicket of golden lotus leaves; Comus of 1911 rode beneath a flowing canopy of cloth-of-gold. The golden minarets of Wilde's Xanadu float that same year were festooned with garlands of golden crescents, her "Lost Pleiad" pageant (1905) ablaze with flaming sunbursts and towers of gold, temples that might have been imagined by Louis Comfort Tiffany.

The Mistick Krewe celebrated its Golden Anniversary in 1906, the first such occasion in the history of Carnival. "The Demon Actors in Milton's 'Paradise Lost'" had been the subject of the krewe's inaugural parade; fifty years later they summoned visions of poetic wealth and sensuality from the source of their august nativity, Milton's *Comus*. Comus, cloaked in gold and diamonds, was enthroned on a car of golden laurels, followed by one of Wilde's finest title designs—an enormous mask of Comus himself, youthful, smiling, and wreathed with clusters of grapes, rose above the banner announcing the theme, "The Masque of Comus." Float number thirteen in this golden pageant illustrated "Nature's Bounties," perhaps Comus's most seductive speech, an exaltation of the senses, and of beauty:

Wherefore did Nature pour her bounties forth,
With such a full and unwithdrawing hand,
Covering the earth with odours, fruits, and flocks,
Thronging the seas with spawn innumerable,
But all to please and sate the curious taste?
And set to work millions of spinning worms,
That in their green shops weave the smooth-
  haired silk
To deck her sons, and that no corner might
Be vacant of her plenty, in her own loins
She hutched the all-worshipped ore and
  precious gems
To store her children with; if all the world
Should in a pet of temperance feed on pulse,
Drink the clear stream, and nothing wear but frieze,
The All-giver would be unthanked, would be
  unpraised,
Not half his riches known, and yet despised,
And we should serve him as a grudging master,

As a penurious niggard of his wealth,
And live like Nature's bastards, not her sons. . . .
Beauty is nature's coin, must not be hoarded,
But must be current, and the good thereof
Consists in mutual and partaken bliss. . . .
Beauty is Nature's brag, and must be shown
In courts, at feasts, and high solemnities
Where most may wonder at the workmanship.

At the Comus anniversary ball, Miss Wilde was again the recipient of a special honor, a crystal replica of the cup carried by Comus, with *Comus* and the date wrought in silver. This triumphant collaboration, with artist and krewe at the peaks of their powers, continued for another eight years. Wilde's spectacular watercolor designs for four of them—"Tennyson" (1907), "Flights of Fancy" (1909), "Familiar Quotations" (1911), and "Tales from Chaucer" (1914)—are preserved at Tulane University. We have only tracings or lithographed

Carnival Bulletins of the others—"Gods and Goddesses" (1908), "Mahomet" (1910), "Cathay" (1912), and "Time's Mysteries" (1913).

"Time's Mysteries" was the last Comus parade Jennie Wilde lived to see. On vacation in England that September, she became ill and sought to convalesce in a Measden convent, where she died on September 11, 1913. Five months later, the Carnival of 1914 was closed with the Comus-Wilde valedictory, "Tales from Chaucer." The last float depicted "Truth," with guardian lions and golden towers rising upon a mound of burning clouds and molten sunbursts. Jennie Wilde was buried in Metairie Cemetery, not far from the imposing tombs of the Comus captains with whom she worked. To her family grave was added a shaft of white marble, designed by Wilde and inscribed *Mizpah*, the Hebrew benediction from Genesis— "God will watch over us when we are apart."

Jennie Wilde, "Comus, No. 1 Car," watercolor float design for Comus pageant, 1892: "Nippon, the Land of the Rising Sun."

Jennie Wilde, "Wraiths of the Rainbow," chromolithograph of float design for
Comus pageant, 1891: "Demonology."

Jennie Wilde, "Vampires of War," chromolithograph of float design for Comus
pageant, 1891: "Demonology."

CARNIVAL EDITION OF THE Picayune

PROCESSION OF THE MISTICK KREWE

NEW ORLEANS 1892 MARCH 1st

Nº 3 O'TENSAN, THE MIKADO.

Nº 4 KONTON, IN THE BEGINNING.

Nº 5 IZANAGI AND IZANAMI, THE FIRST

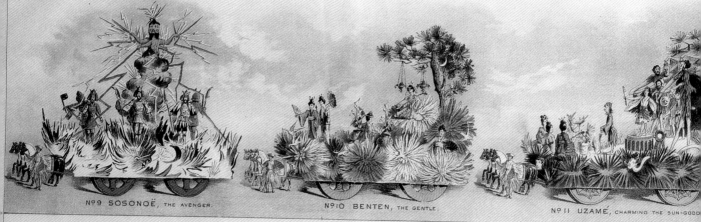

Nº 9 SOSONOË, THE AVENGER.

Nº 10 BENTEN, THE GENTLE.

Nº 11 UZAMÉ, CHARMING THE SUN-GODD

Nº 15 SEKAI-NO, EARTH'S OFFSPRING.

Nº 16 SUI-JIN, FATHER OF FLOODS.

Nº 17 SOZANOO, THE DRAGON CONQ

SUBJECT * NIPPON *
THE LAND OF THE RISING SUN

Nº 1 COMUS.

Nº 2 NIPPON, THE LAND OF THE RISING SUN.

Nº 6 AMATARUSU, THE SUN-QUEEN.

Nº 7 YA-NO-ONNA, SPIRITS OF NIGHT.

Nº 8 HIRUKU, RULER OF THE SEA.

Nº 12 INARI-SAMA, GODDESS OF FOOD

Nº 13 TACHIBANE-HIMÉ, THE IDOL OF THE FLOWERS.

Nº 14 TSURIGANE, VOICES OF THE BELLS.

Nº 18 RAI-JIN, THUNDER GOD.

Nº 19 FU-SHI, THE ELIXIR OF IMMORTALITY.

Nº 20 JIMMU-TENNO

Pages 86-87: Jennie Wilde, "Nippon, the Land of the Rising Sun," Carnival Edition of the Comus pageant, 1892. Chromolithography by Daniel Anton Buechner.

Above: Jennie Wilde, "Comus, No. 1 Car," watercolor float design for Comus pageant, 1903: "A Leaf from the Mahabarata."

Opposite, top: Jennie Wilde, "The Brook," watercolor float design for Comus pageant, 1907: "Tennyson."

Opposite, bottom: Jennie Wilde, "Ring Out, Wild Bells," watercolor float design for Comus pageant, 1907: "Tennyson."

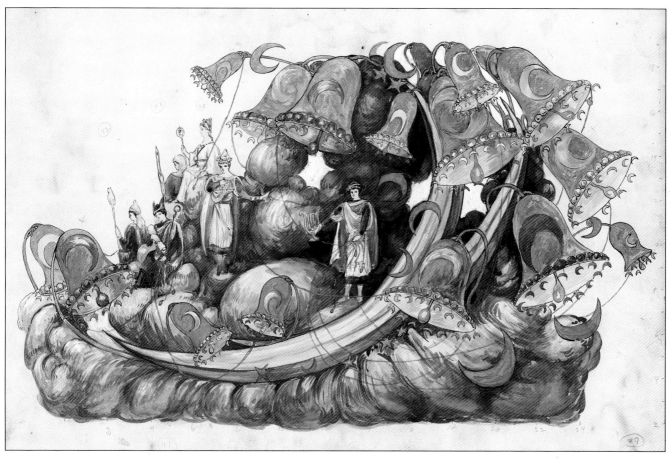

Opposite, top: *Jennie Wilde, "Momus, No. 1 Car," chromolithograph of float design for Momus pageant, 1905: "Vathek, Ninth Caliph of the Abassides."*

Opposite, bottom: *Jennie Wilde, "The Chamber of Horrors," chromolithograph of float design for Momus pageant, 1905: "Vathek, Ninth Caliph of the Abassides."*

Above: *Jennie Wilde, "Title Car," chromolithograph of float design for Comus pageant, 1906: "The Masque of Comus."*

Pages 94-95: *Jennie Wilde, "Tales of the How and Why," Carnival Edition of the Momus pageant, 1915. Chromolithography by Susus Von Ehren.*

Opposite, top: *Jennie Wilde, "Horai, the Land of Mirage," chromolithograph of float design for Momus pageant, 1906: "Leaves from Oriental Literature."*

Opposite, bottom: *Jennie Wilde, "Momus, No. 1 Car," chromolithograph of float design for Momus pageant, 1909: "Signs and Superstitions."*

Above: *Jennie Wilde, "Comus, No. 1 Car," watercolor float design for Comus pageant, 1909: "Flights of Fancy."*

Above: *Jennie Wilde, "Children of Lir," watercolor float design for Comus pageant, 1909: "Flights of Fancy."*

Opposite, top: *Jennie Wilde, "Rhianon's Birds," watercolor float design for Comus pageant, 1909: "Flights of Fancy."*

Opposite, bottom: *Jennie Wilde, "St. George and the Dragon," watercolor float design for Comus pageant, 1909: "Flights of Fancy."*

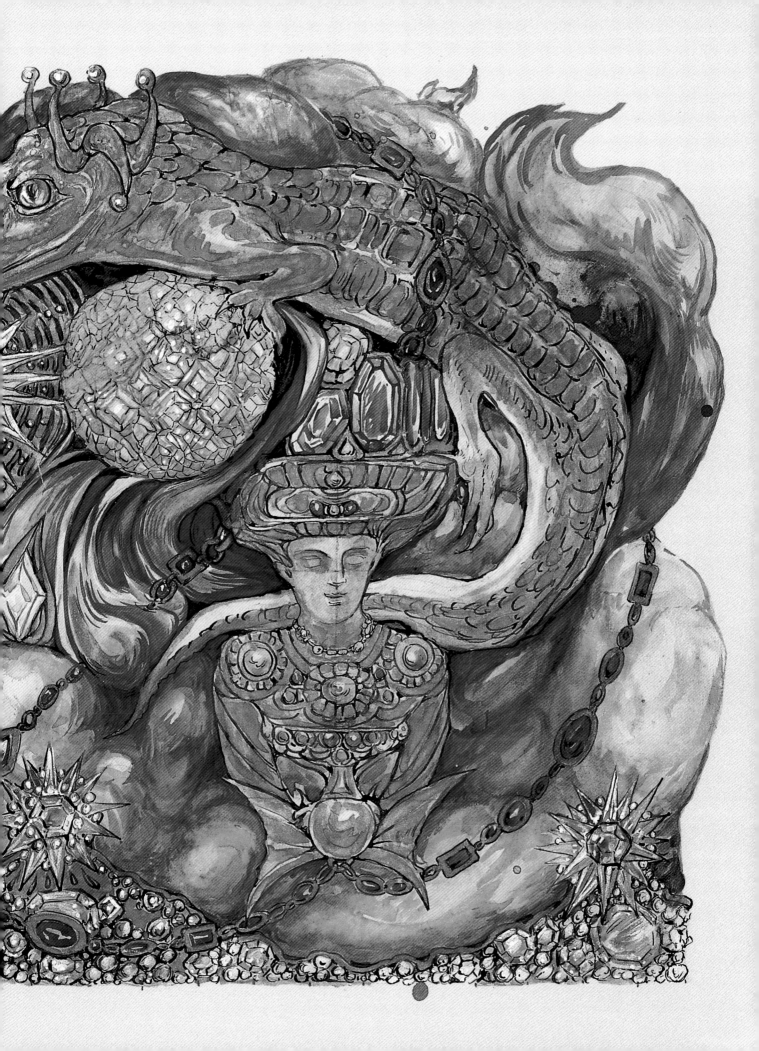

Pages 100-101: *Jennie Wilde, "Prester John," watercolor float design for Comus pageant, 1909: "Flights of Fancy."*

Above: *Jennie Wilde, "Comus, No. 1 Car," watercolor float design for Comus pageant, 1911: "Familiar Quotations."*

Opposite, top: *Jennie Wilde, "The Harp That Once in Tara's Hall," watercolor float design for Comus pageant, 1911: "Familiar Quotations."*

Opposite, bottom: *Jennie Wilde, "What Are the Wild Waves Saying?" watercolor float design for Comus pageant, 1911: "Familiar Quotations."*

Opposite, top: *Jennie Wilde, "The Sunflower Turns," watercolor float design for Comus pageant, 1911: "Familiar Quotations."*

Opposite, bottom: *Jennie Wilde, "The Mills of the Gods Grind Slowly," watercolor float design for Comus pageant, 1911: "Familiar Quotations."*

Above: *Jennie Wilde, "All That Glitters Is Not Gold," watercolor float design for Comus pageant, 1911: "Familiar Quotations."*

Pages 106-7: Jennie Wilde, "In Xanadu Did Xublai Khan," watercolor float design for Comus pageant, 1911: "Familiar Quotations."

Above: Jennie Wilde, "Anelida," watercolor float design for Comus pageant, 1914: "Tales from Chaucer."

Opposite, top: Jennie Wilde, "St. Cecelia," watercolor float design for Comus pageant, 1914: "Tales from Chaucer."

Opposite, bottom: Jennie Wilde, "Pyramis and Thisbe," watercolor float design for Comus pageant, 1914: "Tales from Chaucer."

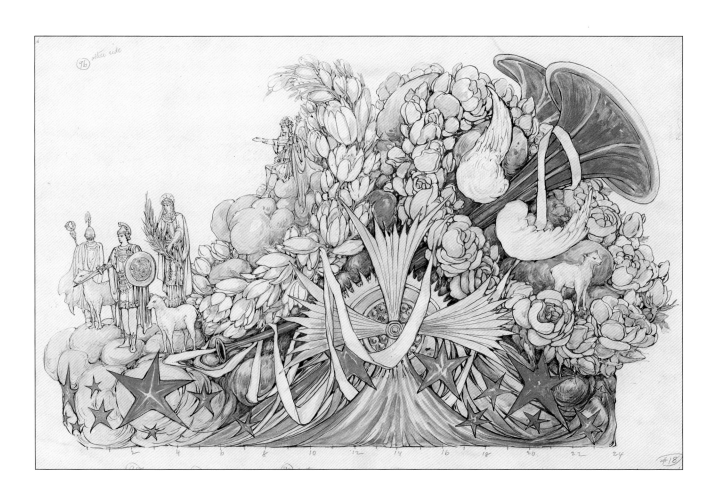

Jennie Wilde, "Truth," watercolor float design for Comus pageant, 1914:
"Tales from Chaucer."

CHAPTER V

BUECHNER, VON EHREN, AND SOULIÉ

Beginning in the mid-1870s, newspaper coverage of the Carnival season began to augment the pageant descriptions with small black and white engravings of the float designs. The evolution of these printed images magically paralleled the increasing grandeur of their subjects, and in 1882 the first large, "broadside" sheets appeared. On one side were the floats for Momus ("The Ramayama"), Proteus ("Ancient Egyptian Theology"), Rex ("The Pursuit of Pleasure"), and Comus ("Worships of the World"); on the other side, amid numerous advertisements, there were explanations and descriptions of the characters and scenes in the arcane tableaux. Lengthy descriptions and thematic explanations also appeared in the daily press, but without illustrations.

The earliest attempts to reproduce the float designs in color came in 1884, with booklets depicting the pageants of Momus ("The Passions"), Proteus ("The Aeneid"), Rex ("The Semitic Races"), and Comus ("Illustrated Ireland"). The color was uneven, and many of the images were out of register, but only two years later, the great wedding of steam presses and color lithography produced the first beautiful chromolithographed Carnival Bulletins—Wikstrom's first complete set of designs for Rex, "Triumph of Aurelian," and Bonnecaze's wondrous "Visions of Other Worlds" for Proteus were reproduced in glorious, saturated color.

Lithography, invented by Alois Senefelder in Germany in 1798, was the first new printing technology since the advent of relief printing in the fifteenth century. The new process was based on the chemical repellence of oil and water. Designs were painted with greasy ink and crayons on specially prepared limestone; the stone was moistened with water, which it accepted in areas not covered by crayon. An oily ink, applied with a roller, adhered only to the drawing and was repelled by the wet parts of the stone; the lithographic print was made by pressing paper against the inked drawing.

During the first half of the nineteenth century, chromolithography remained a relatively expensive process that was used for large-scale folio works (such as John James Audubon's monumental *Birds of America*) or for illuminated books, which often attempted to reproduce the gilded handwork of manuscripts of the Middle Ages. The steam-driven printing press and the wider availability of inexpensive paper stock lowered production costs, and by the early 1880s, the process was widely used in books, magazines, and advertising.

Newspapers, notably the *Times-Democrat* and the *Picayune*, vied with one another to publish the lithographed Carnival Editions. As many as 30,000 of each were printed, and they were always sold separately. These colorful souvenirs could be ordered from the papers, and on the evening of the parades, they were hawked by youngsters on streetcars and street corners for a dime. These ten-cent bulletins have assumed an importance that could not have been imagined when they were produced: because so few collections of original float and costume designs have survived, these lithographs became the visual record of the great processions, with every float from 1877 until the bulletins were discontinued in 1941. The most beautiful examples of the bulletins were the creations of two master lithographers, Daniel Anton Buechner and Susus Von Ehren.

Buechner was born in New Orleans in 1856, but two years later his family moved to Cincinnati, where he was reared and studied art. After beginning his professional career as a lithographer there, in 1872, he began to travel down the Ohio and Mississippi rivers. Following a brief residence in Memphis (where he is listed as that city's first lithographer), Buechner returned to New Orleans in 1877. As a commercial artist with his own studio, Buechner made product designs for the World's Industrial and Cotton Centennial Exposition (1884-85). In 1885 he went to work for the printing firm of T. Fitzwilliam & Co., where he became the premier designer and chromolithographer.

Beginning with "Visions of Other Worlds" in 1886, Buechner created the Fitzwilliam Carnival Bulletins for Momus, Proteus, Phunny Phorty Phellows, Rex, and Comus. While many of these papers have faded over the years, the colors in the best-preserved editions remain stunning—in the atmospheric rendering of the backgrounds and in the vibrant float cartoons. Buechner depicted the wooden float wheels realistically, almost in scale,

and his floats follow one another quietly, across blazing horizons and beneath translucent clouds.

In addition to his accomplishments as a Carnival lithographer, there is the strong likelihood he followed Charles Briton as the designer for the satirical parades of the Phunny Phorty Phellows, and, later, of the Independent Order of the Moon. Buechner created several wonderful invitations for the P.P.P.; and the only Carnival Bulletin ever signed in the plate was the Order's "Moonshine Extra" of 1888, with a large scripted *B* trailing the last float.

Susus Frederick Von Ehren was born in New Orleans around 1866 and, in 1885, he began work as a commercial artist and lithographer for the printing firm of G. Koeckert & Co. Von Ehren, like Buechner, was principally employed to design labels, and in the course of his seventy-year career with one firm, G. Koeckert became Koeckert and Walle, then Walle & Co. Von Ehren's first Carnival work came in illustrating the invitations, proclamations, and bulletins for the revival of the Phunny Phorty Phellows in the late 1890s; it is also likely that he designed the floats. But the work for which he is best remembered are the Carnival Bulletins he created for Walle at the turn of the century, beginning with Rex and Momus in 1902; Comus followed in 1905, Proteus in 1912.

The Von Ehren and Buechner bulletins were alike in size and format, but their stylistic differences were not subtle. Von Ehren's cartoons were more sharply etched, capturing details of the original designs that were often lost with Buechner's crayons. The floats in the Von Ehren bulletins were grouped closer together and also rolled on enormous decorative wheels, which created a semblance of a pageant's dynamic movement. Some of Von Ehren's finest designs and most sumptuous color appeared in the large vignettes identifying the krewe and the subject of each bulletin.

The designs of Briton, Bonnecaze, Wikstrom, and Wilde may be preserved as glorious illustrations in the Carnival Bulletins, but no physical remnant of those Golden Age parades exists today—we have no swag of golden papier-mâché canopy, no ornamental lion head or dragon wing relic. Our documentation rests with vintage photography. Photographs of Rex floats appear as early as 1890, and grow more numerous from the late 1890s. The earliest complete photographic record of parade floats, the 1901 Rex pageant, "Human Passions and Characteristics," was recently discovered in Saratoga Springs, New York, and made a gift to the New Orleans Public Library; but there remains only one known photograph of a nineteenth- or early twentieth-century night parade—"The Devil's Basket" aglow on Canal Street, in the Proteus "Trip to Wonderland" of 1898. These photographs show that the float designs were carefully followed and beautifully finished, brought to life by the reigning production genius of Carnival's Golden Age, Georges Soulié.

Soulié was born in December of 1844 in Paris, where for many years his family constructed pageants for Mardi Gras, and for agricultural festivals in the countryside. He learned the craft of sculpting in plaster and papier-mâché from his father. During the Franco-Prussian War of 1870, Soulié fought in the siege of Paris and was crushed by the outcome. It was soon apparent that the days of pageants and festivities were ended for some time in Paris, and the young artist decided to try his luck in New Orleans.

The ties between Creole New Orleans and Paris were old, and remained strongest in Carnival. The fabulous costumes, jewels, and many of the invitations were made in Paris; and before Soulié, all of the papier-mâché creatures, décors, and masks for Mardi Gras also came from the French capital. The figures were packed into huge crates and shipped to New Orleans, where they would be reassembled and built into the tableaux cars. One of Soulié's first jobs in New Orleans was repairing the damage some props suffered in shipment; another was the commission by the archbishop of New Orleans to construct a large replica of a grotto at Lourdes for the venerable St. Louis Cathedral, in the heart of the old city.

When the design committee for Comus ap-proached Soulié with the designs for "The Missing Links," he convinced them he could transform Briton's fantastic watercolor caricatures into papier-mâché characters, and was awarded the contract. As each of the huge heads was completed, the committee was satisfied with the figure's faithfulness to the design, as well its resemblance in facial features to the intended target. This pageant, the first to be constructed entirely in New Orleans, was an enormous success, and launched a dazzling career that would last more than forty years. Whatever the imaginations of the designers presented, their visions were translated by Soulié's virtuosity.

During this Golden Age of Carnival artistry, each float was newly constructed on a perennial set of chassis. Most of the opulent décors and all of the fabled beasts that populated the pageants were realized in papier-mâché; each float was a piece of sculpted theatrical architecture, upon which skilled carpenters, scenic painters, and decorators also worked their magic. Soulié's work on the floats took place in the hidden warehouses of the krewes (their "dens"), but he also maintained a studio on Exchange Alley, and used the workshop at the French Opera House for Carnival ball décors.

Following the United States entry into World War I all Carnival activities were cancelled; none of the society krewes appeared with parades or balls in 1918 or 1919. In September of 1919, as he refurbished the Rex floats to reappear in the coming Carnival, Georges Soulié died. Though his name is largely forgotten today, Soulié contributed more than any other artist to the development and refinement of the New Orleans Carnival pageants. Soulié was also the founder of a short-lived dynasty—he was succeeded by his son Henry, who, in 1923, formed the partnership Soulié and Crassons, with painter Harry Crassons. Continuing through the cutbacks and financial traumas of the Great Depression, Soulié and Crassons served as float builders for the old-line krewes until the early 1950s.

Nº 1 HIS MAJESTY REX - KING OF THE CARNIVAL

Nº 9 FOUR GODS OF YUCATAN

Opposite, top: *Daniel Anton Buechner, "Rex, No. 1 Car," chromolithograph of float design by Bror Anders Wikstrom for Rex pageant, 1889: "Treasures of the Earth."*

Opposite, bottom: *Daniel Anton Buechner, "Four Gods of Yucatan," chromolithograph of float design for Momus pageant, 1887: "Myths of the New World."*

Above: *Daniel Anton Buechner, "The Sun," chromolithograph of float design by Carlotta Bonnecaze for Proteus pageant, 1886: "Visions of Other Worlds."*

CARNIVAL EDITION of THE Picayune,

EIGHTH Representation Krewe of Prote[us]

1889 VOL. LIV NEW ORLEANS, LA. No 40.

MARCH, 5TH 1889

T. FITZWILLIAM & CO. LITHOGRAPHERS, NEW ORLEANS.

No 1 PROT[eus]

No 4 ENGHA - THE BOAT-MAN.

No 5 DURGA (VIRTUE) SLAYING MAHISHASURA (VICE)

No 6 K[...]

No 7 DEVAS AND ASSURAS

No 10 KUVERA - GOD OF RICHES

No [...]

No 14 VARUNA - GOD OF OCEAN

No 15 GANESA - GOD OF WISDOM.

SUBJECT ✱ THE HINDOO HEAVENS.

Nº2 OAHANA - GODDESS OF MORNING

Nº3 MOHINY - GODDESS OF LOVE

SE OF SIVA

Nº7 SURYA - THE SUN.

Nº8 SATTIA LOCA - PARADISE OF BRAHMA.

OF HELL

Nº12 SWARGA - PARADISE OF INDRA

Nº13 AGNI - GOD OF FIRE.

Nº17 SOMA - THE MOON.

Nº18 KALKI AVATAR

CARNIVAL EDITION OF REX 1889
The Picayune

NEW ORLEANS, LA.

MARCH 5TH 1889.

T. FITZWILLIAM & CO. LITHOGRAPHERS, NEW ORLEANS.

SUBJECT

BOEUF GRAS

Nº 4 RUBIES

Nº 5 SILVER

Nº 9 IRON

Nº 10 MARBLE

Nº 14 IVORY

Nº 15 GOLD

Nº 16 AMETHYSTS

SURES OF THE EARTH.

N°1 HIS MAJESTY REX—KING OF THE CARNIVAL N°2 INTRODUCTORY N°3 PEARLS

LS N°7 FRUIT N°8 CRYSTALS

COPPER N°12 DIAMONDS N°13 SAPPHIRES

N°17 EMERALDS N°18 CORAL N°19 ONYX

2. TITLE CAR   3. DRAWING THE HOROSCOPE   4. THE SACRED SCROLL

TRANGE FRUITS   8. SHERAHIYA THE GIANT   9. BELOUKIYA AND SEKHER

AND OF APES   13. THE THREE DOVE MAIDS   14. JANSHAH

18. THE KING OF THE BEASTS   19. SHEIKH NESR   20. THE CRYSTAL ISLAND

Pages 116-17: *Daniel Anton Buechner, "The Hindoo Heavens," chromolithographed Carnival Edition of designs by Carlotta Bonnecaze for Proteus pageant, 1889.*

Pages 118-19: *Daniel Anton Buechner, "Treasures of the Earth," chromolithographed Carnival Edition of designs by Bror Anders Wikstrom for Rex pageant, 1889.*

Pages 120-21: *Daniel Anton Buechner, "The Queen of the Serpents," chromolithographed Carnival Edition of designs by Bror Anders Wikstrom for Proteus pageant, 1907.*

Above: *Susus Von Ehren, "Agate," chromolithograph of float design by Bror Anders Wikstrom for Rex pageant, 1909: "The Treasures of the King."*

Opposite, top: *Susus Von Ehren, "National Currency," detail of chromolithograph of Carnival Bulletin for Phunny Phorty Phellows pageant, 1896: "Phads and Phancies."*

Opposite, bottom: *Susus Von Ehren, "Phad of Creation," detail of chromolithograph of Carnival Bulletin for Phunny Phorty Phellows pageant, 1896: "Phads and Phancies."*

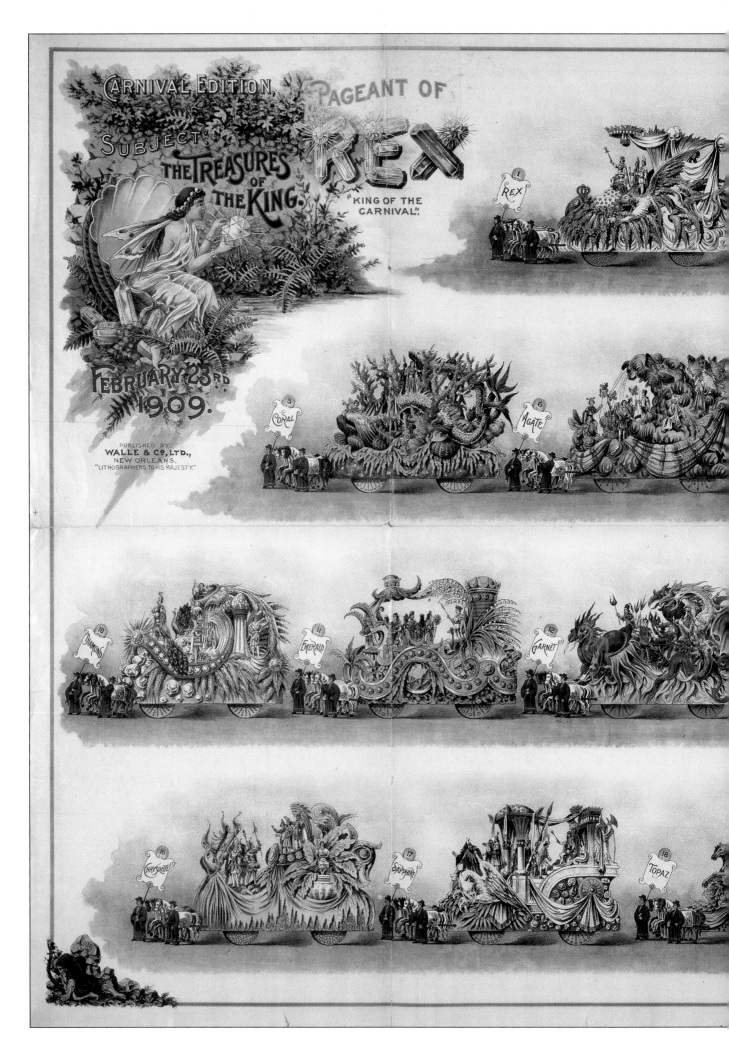

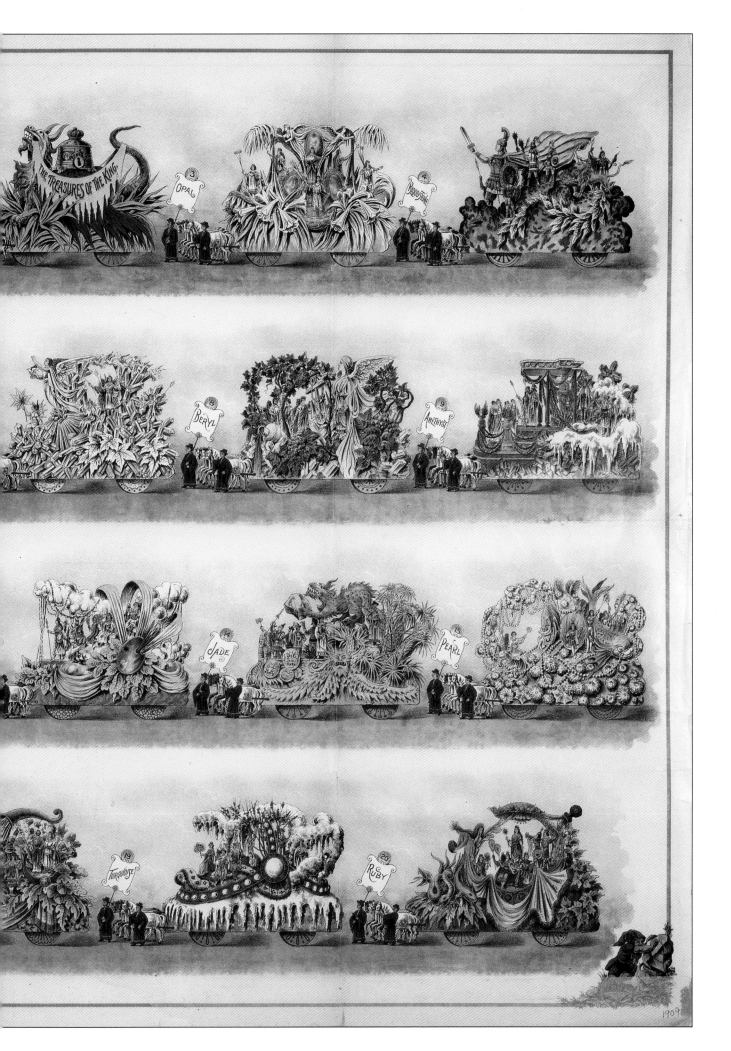

THE TREASURES OF THE KING

3 OPAL

4 BLOODSTONE

8 BERYL

9 AMETHYST

14 JADE

15 PEARL

19 TURQUOISE

20 RUBY

1909

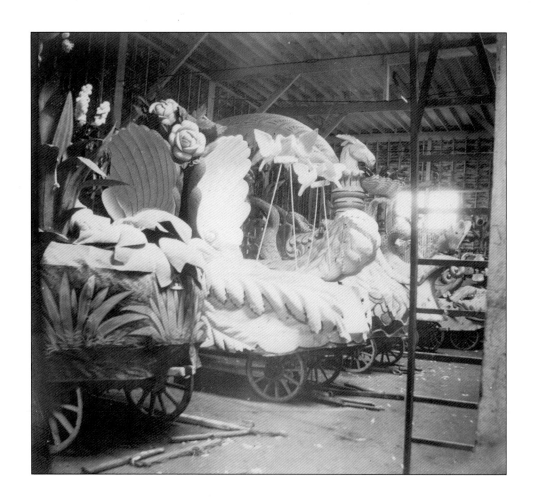

Pages 124-25: Susus Von Ehren, "The Lost Pleiad," chromolithographed Carnival
Edition of designs by Jennie Wilde for Comus pageant, 1905.

Pages 126-27: Susus Von Ehren, "In Utopia," chromolithographed Carnival
Edition of designs by Bror Anders Wikstrom for Rex pageant, 1906.

Pages 128-29: Susus Von Ehren, "The Treasures of the King," chromolithographed
Carnival Edition of designs by Bror Anders Wikstrom for Rex pageant, 1909.

Opposite, top: Cornelius Durkee, "Rex Floats in Their Den," February 1901. This
remarkable image is the only known vintage photograph of a Carnival den interior.

Opposite, bottom: Anon., silver gelatin print showing the Georges Soulié workshop, perhaps in the basement of the French Opera House.

Above: Anon., silver gelatin print, "Comus Floats Outside Den, Mardi Gras
Afternoon," with workers and tableaux signs for pageant, 1896: "The Months and
Seasons of the Year."

*Anon., hand-tinted postcard of Bror Anders Wikstrom, "Abode of Enchantment," float
for Rex pageant, 1904: "In the Realm of the Imagination." Built by Georges Soulié.*

*Susus Von Ehren, "Abode of Enchantment," chromolithograph of float design by
Bror Anders Wikstrom for Rex pageant, 1904: "In the Realm of the Imagination."*

John Teunisson, tinted postcard of Bror Anders Wikstrom, "Season of the Feathered Songsters," float for Rex pageant, 1904: "In the Realm of the Imagination." Built by Georges Soulié.

Susus Von Ehren, "Season of the Feathered Songsters," chromolithograph of float design by Bror Anders Wikstrom for Rex pageant, 1904: "In the Realm of the Imagination."

Above: *Anon. of Ceneilla Bower Alexander, "Rex, No. 1 Car," float for Rex pageant, 1917: "Gifts of the Gods to Louisiana." Built by Georges Soulié.*

Below: *"Phoebus from His Molten Gold Gives Sunshine."*

Above: Anon. of Ceneilla Bower Alexander, "Mercury Ordains Transportation," float for Rex pageant, 1917: "Gifts of the Gods to Louisiana." Built by Georges Soulié.

Below: "Oceanus Dips from the Depths Our Salt."

Above: *Georges Soulié, letterhead (circa 1890), depicting a glorious procession of floats returning to their heavenly den. In a career that spanned more than forty years, Georges Soulié was the reigning production genius of Carnival's Golden Age.*

Below: *Anon. of Louis Andrews Fischer, "Love in China," float for Rex pageant, 1921: "Porcelain in Fact and Fancy." Built by Henry Soulié.*

CHAPTER VI

ALEXANDER, FISCHER, AND PLAUCHÉ

ikstrom's successor as designer for Rex was Ceneilla Bower Alexander. Mrs. Alexander, as she was known throughout her career, may have designed as few as ten parades, but they formed the last substantial body of work begun in the glorious years before the First World War. Like Jennie Wilde, Alexander was a native of Georgia, and both women were born in 1865. Ceneilla Bower studied at the New York School of Art in Manhattan, and later married William McFadden Alexander, a Presbyterian minister. Mrs. Alexander's first Carnival works of record were watercolor costume plates for the Krewe of Nereus in 1897, beautifully drawn and delicately colored, her abiding hallmarks. None of the Carnival designers surpassed her in draftsmanship; only the palest blushes of color were applied to her virtuoso pen and ink designs, maelstroms of energy and imagination. Like Wilde, she seemed to nurse a horror of the void. No surface lacked ornament, and her depictions of air and water swirled into the dreamy depths of old mirrors reflecting one another.

Alexander's float plates were aglow with shameless luxury and flamboyant excess, ancient allies of Mardi Gras, and while only two sets of her designs for Rex have survived, each offers examples of her most amazing work. "Phases of Nature" (in 1912) began with "The Reign of Darkness," "The Creation of Light," and "The Rising of the Mists," with echoes of Wikstrom's "Rubaiyat"; but in "The Awakening Year," "The Cataract," and "The Whirlpool," Alexander's fluid pen began to dance.

In the title car for "The Drama of the Year" (1914) we encounter Alexander's most complex and beautifully layered illustration. The subject (originally titled "The Dream of the Hour: A Fantasy") appeared on a golden ribbon, high above a blazing sunburst. At the back of the float, atop a mound of star-studded clouds, rose a golden being wearing a helmet of sunbursts and a mask; sheathed in golden armor, this mysterious sun-creature's arm pushed a papier-mâché globe across the top of the float, with the moon and a shower of stars trailing in its flight. Masks appeared half-lowered on amorphous faces, smiling and glaring, and masks unworn, perhaps discarded, were woven into an extravagant dreamscape of veils, garlands of jewels, and gleaming dragon tails.

As illustrations, designs for "The Drama of the Year" have retained all of their sumptuous guile and ready charm, and many of them were transformed into opulent papier-mâché tableaux. But many of the details, as well as the layers of diaphanous fabrics and translucent mists, went unrealized by sculptor or decorator. To the artists commissioned to build what she had designed, Alexander must have seemed possessed; float plates were accompanied by lengthy scribbled notes of instructions, interpreting every symbol in the designs, explaining their importance, demanding their executions. The costume plates were lightened with gestures of wit and mischief, but their reverse sides were also covered with choruses of explication and exasperation. She had little regard for Georges or Henry Soulié, and less for the scenic painting of Harry Crassons.

A rapturous, watery throne setting for the 1923 Rex parade was her final float plate: on the ocean floor, amid rolling waves and garlands of pearls, rose a circular pedestal, sculpted in full relief with classical female caryatids, their arms raised to support the throne platform. On it sat Rex, inside a large scallop festooned with seaweed and more pearls; from a point above the king, arches of seabirds, fore and aft, curved to the four corners of the float. The arches of seabirds also appeared in the Carnival Bulletin, but they were the only element in the fantasy that is absent in photographs, a detail that would have invoked Alexander's wrath. Mrs. Alexander was the lone diva among the Carnival artists, and her ongoing disdain for her collaborators may have contributed to her retirement. She died at the age of 101 in 1966, and her obituaries credited her with designs that, in fact, postdated her activity.

The glory days of Carnival's Golden Age were interrupted by World War I and ended with the burning of the French Opera House in December of 1919. Rex alone appeared in the 1920 season; Proteus did not return until 1922; Momus, 1923; Comus, 1924. The destruction of the French Opera also dramatized the changes under way in theatrical venues. In New Orleans, as everywhere else, theatergoers were lining up for movies, and an army of skilled scenic artists was forced to seek other employment.

The picturesque buildings of the French Quarter, as it was beginning to be called, continued to fascinate young artists and writers, and in the 1920s the old sector became home to a distinguished literary circle. Sherwood Anderson, the Pulitzer Prize-winning novelist, was the group's leading light; in 1921 two young natives, Albert Goldstein and Julius Friend, founded *The Double Dealer,* in which they published works by the as yet unknown Hart Crane, Ernest Hemingway, William Faulkner, and Edmund Wilson. Faulkner lived in the French Quarter, and wrote his first novel, *Soldier's Pay,* in an apartment overlooking the garden behind St. Louis Cathedral. As co-author, he wrote the introduction to *Sherwood Anderson and Other Famous Creoles,* a small book of forty drawings by William Spratling, containing caricatures of artists, writers, and personalities of the Vieux Carré. Among them was Louis Andrews Fischer.

That we can now appreciate one artist for then maintaining Carnival's canon is, perhaps, unremarkable; that she repeated the task more than thirty years later, in more desultory times, is cause for wonder. Louis Andrews Fischer began her Carnival work while still a student at Newcomb College in 1921, illustrating a booklet for the Momus ball, "The Battle of Don Carnival with Lady Lent." The following year she designed the Rex and Proteus parades, and continued to work for Rex through 1932. An exuberant classicist, Louis Andrews Fischer was the first Carnival designer born in the twentieth century, and her early work reflected many eclectic influences—of her immediate predecessors, the Arts and Crafts Movement, art deco illustration, and Bakst designs for the Ballets Russes. But none of them shaped her style more than her lifelong loves, literature and nonsense.

Louis Andrews was born on February 22, 1901 in Mobile, Alabama, the cradle of Carnival pageantry; she was given her father's name, Louis. Five years later, following the birth of her sister, Martha, their father left Mrs. Andrews and they were divorced. Louis Andrews was a bright child, but also singularly unattractive, a curse she never escaped; Mrs. Andrews dressed her homely daughter in tailored clothes and boyish suits.

Five years after the birth of the beautiful Martha, Mrs. Andrews moved with her daughters to New

Orleans, and to the Pontalba apartments in the Vieux Carré. Young Louis Andrews showed early talent in drawing and a love of books, and both interests were nourished. Mrs. Andrews was devoted to poetry, particularly the work of Alexander Pope, and many of her admonitions were accompanied by couplets of his verse. Louis, from childhood, was devoted to Lewis Carroll's "Alice" books and to the nonsense verse of Edward Lear. At sixteen, she entered Newcomb College, where she excelled.

Her first float designs were for the Proteus parade of 1922, "The Romance of the Rose," an impressive synthesis of medieval illumination, art deco foliage, and Jennie Wilde motifs. Against a sky of black, a startling innovation of design, Proteus was drawn by a flock of delicately hued butterflies, followed by scenes of "Sir Mirth's Garden," "Love and Reason," "Night's Jeweled Candles," and "Love Conquers All." When Momus returned in 1923, his pageant was designed by Louis Andrews and the subject was "Alice's Adventures in Wonderland and Through the Looking Glass." After her marriage to Lawrence Fischer in 1926, they continued to live in the Pontalba, where for decades they hosted frequent gatherings of friends, and encouraged fledgling members of the artistic, literary, and theatrical communities. The Rex and Momus parades of the early 1930s were the last designed by Fischer for more than thirty years; from her return in 1964 until her death in 1974, she designed the pageants of Comus, Momus, and Proteus. During the lengthy interregnum of her float work, Fischer continued to design costumes and ball settings for the old-line as well as many of the new krewes.

Of all the float designers, none was more steeped in love of the Carnival than Leda Hincks Plauché, a member of an old Creole family. Leda Hincks was born in New Orleans on December 30, 1886; she studied at Newcomb College, and in 1906 was married to Henry Ovid Plauché, an eminent Creole, future president of the New Orleans Cotton Exchange, and a Mardi Gras "extraordinaire"—Henry Plauché served as captain of the Atlanteans, one of Carnival's smallest and most exclusive krewes, for forty years, and as member or chairman of the court committees at countless Carnival balls. Costume designs for the Krewe of Nereus in 1916

were among Leda Plauché's first Carnival work, and she exhibited at the Art Association of New Orleans in 1917.

Her debut as a float designer came with Proteus in 1923, "Myths and Legends of the North America Indians." "Neta-Tua" was the Proteus theme for 1924, with wonders like "The Plot of Abi," with an enormous papier-mâché octopus wrapped around the back of the float, its tentacles overturning a large urn of blood. The year after Comus returned to Mardi Gras, his subject was "The Realms of Phantasy," in which Jennie Wilde's designs for "Flights of Fancy" were recreated float by float, in the exact order in which they had appeared in the Comus parade of 1909. "Flights of Fancy" had left the den in threatening weather and was quickly engulfed by torrential rains. The Comus captain's decision to resurrect Wilde's designs may have been an attempt to right the 1909 calamity, but it more likely was shaped by economic considerations. Princely spending on Carnival continued, but rarely with the profligate hand of the Belle Epoque. World War I not only interrupted Carnival, it gave birth to a Mardi Gras nemesis, the income tax.

With the coming of the Great Depression, the curtain on the Golden Age of Carnival parade artistry was lowered with an emphatic thud. When the stock market collapsed on Black Tuesday, October 29, 1929, work on the pageants of the coming season was nearing completion. On Mardi Gras morning of 1930, Rex presented a lavish production, "The Jewels of Rex" (designs by Louis Fischer); the subject chosen by Comus was "The Legend of Faust" (designs by Leda Plauché).

These parades were followed by years of financial difficulties and cutbacks. Momus failed to appear from 1932 to 1935, and when he returned in 1936 it was with two fewer floats; the number of floats in the Comus procession fell from twenty to seventeen. These economies gave birth to new traditions, perhaps the most important being the evolution of the kings' floats that became Carnival icons, all three of them designed by Plauché—the throne of Proteus, rising above the waves in a pink scallop, and the golden canopies of Rex and Comus. With the addition of the Momus designs to her drawing board, Plauché became the first artist since Briton to design the four major Mardi Gras pageants for multiple seasons.

Plauché's French Quarter studio was also her Royal Street shop, the Green Orchid. Amid the souvenirs and novelties that were for sale, there was a display of Carnival treasures no one could buy; royal regalia Plauché had designed, including the gowns her daughter Myldred had worn in 1930 as queen of Atlanteans and queen of Proteus, were fitted onto mannequins. Beneath their frozen gazes, on a stage ringed with gilded balusters, were miniature replicas of Plauché's floats for the 1924 parade of Proteus, "Neta-Tua," a romance of old Egypt.

Above: *Ceneilla Bower Alexander, "Monday King," watercolor float design for the Monday arrival pageant of Rex, 1913.*

Opposite, top: *Ceneilla Bower Alexander, "The Cataract," watercolor float design for Rex pageant, 1912: "Phases of Nature."*

Opposite, bottom: *Ceneilla Bower Alexander, "The Awakening Year," watercolor float design for Rex pageant, 1912: "Phases of Nature."*

Opposite, top: *Ceneilla Bower Alexander, "The Glory of Summer," watercolor float design for Rex pageant, 1914: "The Drama of the Year."*

Opposite, bottom: *Ceneilla Bower Alexander, "Rhapsody of the March Wind," watercolor float design for Rex pageant, 1914: "The Drama of the Year."*

Above: *Ceneilla Bower Alexander, "Title Car," watercolor float design for Rex pageant, 1914: "The Drama of the Year." (Working title "The Dream of the Hour: A Fantasy.")*

Ceneilla Bower Alexander, "The Drought," watercolor float design for Rex pageant, 1912: "Phases of Nature."

*Ceneilla Bower Alexander, "Rex, No. 1 Car," watercolor float design for
Rex pageant, 1923: "A Fantasy of the Sea."*

Opposite, top: *Louis Andrews Fischer, "Proteus, No. 1 Car," watercolor float design for Proteus pageant, 1922: "The Romance of the Rose."*

Opposite, bottom: *Louis Andrews Fischer, "Love Conquers All," watercolor float design for Proteus pageant, 1922: "The Romance of the Rose."*

Above: *Louis Andrews Fischer, "Title Car," watercolor float design for Momus pageant, 1923: "Alice's Adventures in Wonderland and Through the Looking Glass."*

Above: *Louis Andrews Fischer, title unknown, watercolor float design of the Ballets Russes, circa 1925.*

Opposite, top: *Louis Andrews Fischer, "Rex, No. 1 Car," preliminary pencil drawing for Rex pageant, 1930: "The Jewels of Rex."*

Opposite, middle: *Louis Andrews Fischer, "Title Car," preliminary pencil drawing for Rex pageant, 1930: "The Jewels of Rex."*

Opposite, bottom: *Louis Andrews Fischer, "Japanese Rock Crystal," float design for Rex pageant, 1930: "The Jewels of Rex."*

ct 🍃

s of **Rex**

NEW ORLEANS

New Orleans

Tuesday, March 4th
1930

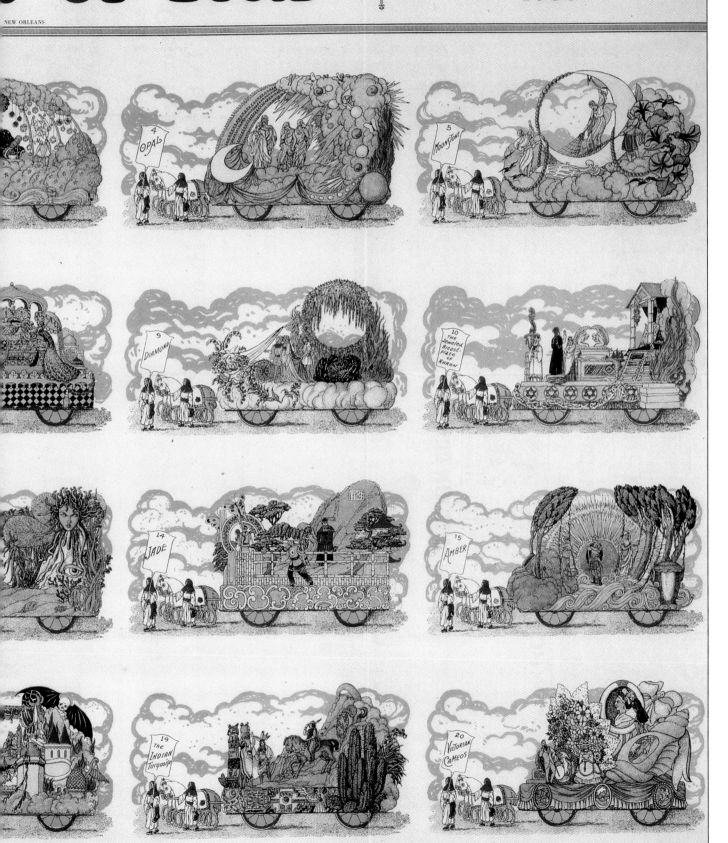

5   6   7   8   9

Pages 150-51: *Louis Andrews Fischer, "The Jewels of Rex," Carnival Edition of the Rex pageant, 1930. Printed by Searcy and Phaff, New Orleans.*

Opposite, top: *Leda Hincks Plauché, "The Trysting Place of Lovers," watercolor float design for Proteus pageant, 1924: "Neta-Tua."*

Opposite, bottom: *Leda Hincks Plauché, "The Plot of Abi," watercolor float design for Proteus pageant, 1924: "Neta-Tua."*

Above: *Leda Hincks Plauché, "The Palace of the Ocean Bed," watercolor float design for Proteus pageant, 1925: "Tales and Romances of Old Japan."*

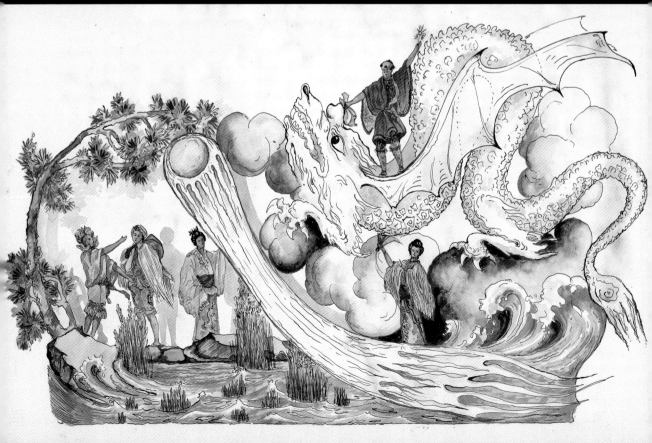

Opposite, top: *Leda Hincks Plauché, "Susa-No-Wo, Dragon of the Sea," watercolor float design for Proteus pageant, 1925: "Tales and Romances of Old Japan."*

Opposite, bottom: *Leda Hincks Plauché, "Rai Taro, the Son of the Thunder God," watercolor float design for Proteus pageant, 1925: "Tales and Romances of Old Japan."*

Above: *Leda Hincks Plauché, "God of Autumn and God of Spring," watercolor float design for Proteus pageant, 1925: "Tales and Romances of Old Japan."*

The Legen

SEARCY & PFAF

INDEX

ACKNOWLEDGMENTS

I would first like to acknowledge the importance of Special Collections, Tulane University, to this project. The great majority of the material pictured in this book is housed there, and I am indebted to Dr. Wilbur Meneray, director, for his cooperation. For their kind and ongoing assistance, I would also like to thank the collection staff members: Mary LeBlanc, Leon Miller, Courtney Page, Carol Hampshire, Kenneth Owen, Ann Case, Dr. Joan Caldwell, and Dr. Robert Sherer.

At the Louisiana State Museum I would like to thank director James F. Sefcik for his cooperation, and to acknowledge the patient assistance of Wayne Phillips, curator of Carnival, and Shannon Glasheen, acting registrar. I am grateful to Priscilla Lawrence, director of The Historic New Orleans Collection, to curator John Magill, and to photographer Jan Brantley for their help. I would like to thank Collin Hamer and Wayne Eberhard of the Louisiana Collection at the New Orleans Public Library for permission to use the Cornelius Durkee photograph. I would also like to thank Philip Biondillo, Jr., Arthur Hardy, Sidney Hebert, and Blaine Kern for their generosity with their collections.

In the production of this book I would like to acknowledge Owen Murphy's photography and Rene Vicedomini's scans at Orleans Colour. John Kelly's research assistance was invaluable, as was Jon Newlin's work on the index. At Pelican Publishing, I would like to acknowledge Dr. Milburn Calhoun's ongoing enthusiasm for this series of *Mardi Gras Treasures*. It has remained a pleasure to work with editor Nina Kooij, designer Tracey Clements, secretary Sally Boitnott, and typesetter Gwynn Harris.

PICTURE CREDITS